# A Brief History of Philosophy

Also available from Continuum:

*What Philosophy Is*, edited by Havi Carel and David Gamez

*What Philosophers Think*, edited by Julian Baggini and
Jeremy Stangroom

*Great Thinkers A–Z*, edited by Julian Baggini and
Jeremy Stangroom

# A Brief History of Philosophy

## From Socrates to Derrida

**Derek Johnston**

continuum
LONDON • NEW YORK

Continuum
The Tower Building
11 York Road
London SE1 7NX

80 Maiden Lane
Suite 704
New York, NY 10038

Illustrated by John Sunderland (johnsam@o2.ie).

British Library Cataloguing-in-Publication Data
A catalogue record for this book is available from the British Library.

ISBN:   HB: 0-8264-9019-0
        PB: 0-8264-9020-4

Library of Congress Cataloging-in-Publication Data
A catalog record for this book is available from the Library of Congress.


Typeset by Servis Filmsetting Ltd, Manchester
Printed and bound in Great Britain by MPG Books Ltd, Bodmin, Cornwall

For June,
with love

# Contents

# List of figures

# Introduction

You have picked up a philosophy book, so you are interested in finding out what philosophy is about. People use the word 'philosophy' in many different ways. Thinking in the abstract might be one way of looking at it. A set of basic ideas which guide my everyday living might be another. What I want to get out of life is a third way of using the word. Those are all definitions of philosophy which are drawn from the realm of everyday experience. Philosophy (with a capital P) is a discipline concerned with thinking, but even professional philosophers do not always agree on a common definition.

## What is philosophy?

There is no one definition of philosophy adopted in this book. What you will find are examples of how significant philosophers have approached this subject. Most of the main branches of philosophy are mentioned at some stage.

*Epistemology* is that area of philosophy that asks how we know things. When are we entitled to say we know? What does the word 'know' mean? Look at the word 'know' as it is used in a number of different sentences:

    I know that two and two make four.
    I know that the earth goes around the sun.
    I know John.
    I know London well.
    I know how to use an ATM.
    I know there are fifteen people in the room.

Sometimes 'know' refers to acquaintance and familiarity, to a skill, to the application of a rule, to something I have personally checked.

Sometimes it refers to a fixed unchanging reality, sometimes to a temporary, volatile state of affairs. All these meanings are subtly different.

*Logic* is concerned with the rules we need in order to think carefully and confidently, and about how and when we ought to apply them.

*Metaphysics* refers to the study of being as being. It is concerned with first principles and causes. It tries to apply reason to the things that go beyond us, studying things in themselves. It is a difficult word to explain. It is best to see examples scattered throughout the text of how and when it is used.

*Ethics* is concerned with right and wrong. Which actions are right, which are wrong? How do I know? What are the correct goals in life and what are the correct ways of going about them? If my goals and intentions are correct, does it matter how I go about achieving them? What are my duties and obligations?

*Political philosophy* is a branch of ethics and is concerned with how we live together as communities. It studies forms of government and examines who is entitled to make laws and where that entitlement comes from. What are the duties and obligations of the citizen and of the state? What are the rights of the citizen? What is the connection between rights and responsibilities? Who is entitled to exercise power over other persons and in what circumstances?

*Aesthetics* is concerned with art and beauty and with human responses to them.

These are some of the main divisions of philosophy, but many more could be added: philosophy of science is one example. Many theoretical and technical disciplines were once considered part of philosophy but have, with the passage of time, become quite independent: one might mention psychology, mathematics and linguistics.

You will by now have noticed that we talk a great deal about the sort of questions that philosophers ask. There is much less about the answers they give. Of course not all philosophers agree about many of the answers that have been proposed. What is more, they are not always agreed about what questions should take priority. That is part of the eternal fascination of philosophy: there seems to be no prospect of coming to a point where it will be said, 'That's it! The matter has been decided once and for all.' In that case, is it worth bothering about? Here philosophers are agreed: yes, it is. But why is philosophy worth bothering about? Here again different thinkers give different answers, so it is up to you to formulate an answer to that question as you read. Here I shall give just two reasons: in every sphere of life the proposals placed before us should always be examined critically; in addition, we should be prepared to think differently.

A word about methodology. Philosophers do not proceed in a haphazard, uncontrolled way. They never say, 'I just don't feel like agreeing with you, so I'm not going to and there is nothing you can do about it. So there!' Philosophy is about discipline and about being clear and reasonable. Philosophy is about considering, thinking deeply about a problem, and about criticism, judging carefully. Criticism is not a negative word: it is about weighing up and coming to a reasoned conclusion. Reason is the operative word – we are not talking about movements of humour.

## What you will find in this book

This book is about fifteen world-famous philosophers. Each one of them has in some way made a major contribution to philosophy or changed the way in which we think about philosophy. They often began their philosophical careers by criticizing a philosopher who had gone before them. Many of them would never in a thousand years agree on a definition of philosophy, such is the divergence in their thinking.

Anybody knowing anything about philosophy will pick up this book and say, 'That's a ridiculous selection, I would never have chosen those fifteen! He never even mentions so and so!' And I agree. So why this fifteen?

When choosing which philosophers to include I had three criteria in mind. Firstly, I wanted to write an easily accessible introduction to the major philosophical thinkers of the Western tradition, so I tried to include at least one thinker from a broad sweep of philosophical tendencies. There couldn't be too many, so I hit on the number fifteen as being manageable, providing variety and allowing some development of thought, rather than just giving a quick digest of principal ideas. I have occasionally cheated; some chapters cover two thinkers. (Scratch any philosopher and you will not find him as rigorous as he fondly imagines himself to be!) But the fifteen chapters also allow space to hint at an appraisal of the ideas put forward, for one is not doing philosophy unless one is actively involved in critical thought.

Secondly, I wanted to introduce the central concepts in a number of philosophical fields, so I selected the philosophers who might help me do that. Thirdly, I followed my own personal preference, awareness and knowledge. I will not say that I am sympathetic to all the philosophers included – one or two bore me to tears – but they all appear to me to have made interesting contributions to the way we think in the Western world, to have shaped our awareness and to have helped make us what we are.

Many will be disappointed and indignant over what I have left out; all I can say is that this is the selection I have made and I hope that many readers will find it useful, stimulating, and in time go on to fill in the gaps for themselves. I believe the criteria I have used might be described as 'justified subjectivity'!

I have tried as far as possible to give each chapter the same structure. First, there is an introduction to the thinker and the times in which he lived. Next we take a brief look at the life of the thinker. But when dealing with philosophers it is the ideas that are important. So the bulk of the chapter will be devoted to ideas.

A philosopher's main ideas are often developed slowly and over several different books or sets of writing, so these are classified under headings. There are in addition short summaries (in boxes) of the main ideas of certain key texts by various thinkers.

Throughout the various chapters, key ideas and vocabulary associated with each philosopher's thought are dealt with (in boxes which give quick explanations as you read). Definitions are repeated throughout to avoid too much page-turning. Although it is laid out in chronological order, this book is designed so that you can pick it up and start anywhere. Technical terms are kept to a minimum, but are explained as and when they do occur.

There is a 'timeline' for each philosopher. This gives the important episodes in his life and lists his main works, but reference is also made to other philosophical, literary and artistic works being produced at the time, in addition to scientific discoveries and historical events.

Each chapter ends with an appraisal. This is not designed to settle matters once and for all, but will suggest ways in which you might accept or reject ideas, and start thinking as a philosopher.

You will have noticed that no women feature in this work. Women have not yet been recognized as innovators in the Western philosophical canon, but they are coming to prominence in philosophy. Philosophy did not stop yesterday and does not stop today. One of the exciting and interesting things about the philosophy of the future will be the contribution brought to it by women philosophers. This development is already true of theology in particular, where women are now making a significant contribution.

Philosophy is an ongoing process of judging the way people think and opening up possibilities of 'thinking differently'. This is the adventure to which, hopefully, this book calls you. But this work is only a beginning. It may take time and effort, but I hope it will be fun.

# 1  Socrates and Plato: the Fire and the Sun

It has been said that Plato was the first person to provide a theoretical justification for the modern totalitarian state and for the traditional boys' boarding school. (And all of this in the fourth century BCE) However, he did much more than this: he was the first to propose a theory of knowledge and he, or Socrates, first proposed using reason to decide moral questions.

## Ancient Greece

Before we start on our philosophical journey we should look at the background out of which three of the world's greatest philosophers came: ancient Greece. It was a small and harsh land, full of high mountains and with few fertile plains. It bred an independent, hardy, healthy people. The easiest way to travel was by sea. Cities were in close proximity to each other, but cut off by difficult terrain. The Greeks probably had few vegetables and no great variety of fruit. Fish was not as plentiful as in northern lands; meat was most likely to be goat meat. There were olive trees, so olive oil was plentiful as was wine. The climate was sunny, fiercely so in summer, yet without the humidity that saps energy. This land bred a people who were 'tough, active, enterprising and intelligent'.

The ancient Greeks did not live in a national state, as we do today. Each city was an independent unit. The city of Athens was a state of probably 240,000 people, many of them slaves. It was governed by a democratic assembly of free citizens, and famous for its architecture, music, literature and philosophy. The city of Sparta could not have been more different. It was a harsh military state. Even young children were taken away from their homes and brought up in a military environment. Sparta did not value literature, architecture or the arts.

Economic life was carried on by slave labour, while male citizens were trained exclusively for war.

## Socrates

We cannot think about Plato, one of the greatest thinkers of all time, unless we first consider his friend and teacher Socrates. Socrates is considered one of the great saints of philosophy and one of its earliest martyrs. His insistence on truth and on being honest about himself led to his execution. He was charged with corrupting the youth of the city of Athens, of not worshipping the city gods and of introducing new gods.

---

**Timeline**

(All dates are BCE: Before Common Era.)

c. 470  Birth of Socrates

460  Construction of the Temple of Zeus at Olympia

458  Production of *Orestes* by Aeschylus

c. 450  Composition of the *Song of Songs* of the Old Testament
          The Twelve Tables: the earliest codification of Roman law
          La Tène Iron Age Celtic culture in Europe

447–432  Construction of the Acropolis, including the Parthenon, in
              Athens

431–404  Peloponnesian war between Sparta and Athens

430–420  Socrates marries somewhere in this period

430  Production of *Oedipus Rex* by Sophocles

420–399  Socrates famous as a teacher

404  End of the Athenian empire

399  Trial and execution of Socrates

---

## Life

Socrates must have been born around 470 BCE. (We know he died in 399 BCE.) He lived his early life in the great days of Athens, a city at the height of its influence and its cultural flowering. He served as a hoplite in the Athenian army. He was apparently physically ugly. One witness described him as looking like a satyr. Another said he walked like a waterfowl and rolled his eyes. He wore the same garment winter and summer and he always went barefoot. He could remain for long periods of time without moving, and in the most uncomfortable of postures. These were apparently long periods of mental abstraction or concentration. The Delphic oracle said that no one alive was wiser than he. Socrates himself decided that he was wise because he knew that he knew nothing. He was a somewhat sarcastic moral philosopher. His chief tactic was to question people as to how they knew they were right. He was not a builder of a philosophical system, rather he criticized heavily the thinking of others. He is credited with being the first to promote the notion of ethics (deciding on the correct goals for a life and on the correct ways of setting out to achieve them). He himself said that inner conscience never told him what to do; it spoke to him if what he was proposing to do was wrong. The tradition has come down to us that his wife Xanthippe had a very sharp tongue and was not afraid to use it

---

**Satyr**: An ugly demi-god inhabiting rural areas: half-man, half-goat. His body was covered in hairs. He was supposed to have an extreme interest in sexual matters.

**Hoplite**: A heavily armed Greek foot-soldier drawn evidently from the wealthier classes as they had to provide their own equipment.

**Demon or Daemon**: The name Socrates gave to his inner voice, which told him that what he was about to do was wrong.

**Delphic Oracle**: There was an important temple to the Greek god Apollo at Delphi. The priestess there gave people messages said to have been inspired by the god.

on him. On the other hand she may have had much to endure in her life with him.

## Cultural background

Athens in Socrates' youth was rich, powerful and inventive. It had a democratic constitution and was ruled by public-spirited aristocrats. People pleaded their own cases before the courts where the judges were chosen by lot; therefore it was very important to be able to speak convincingly. In the fifth century BCE a class of wandering teachers who would teach the art of persuasive rhetoric became famous. They were known as Sophists: professional teachers who trained young men for political life. They could on occasion use their skill in an unscrupulous way. By and large they were indifferent to religion, moral considerations or the philosophical way of life. The Sophist Protagoras taught, 'Man is the measure of all things, of things that are that they are, of things that are not that they are not.' People understood this to mean that there were no independent truths: one person's opinion was as good as another's. Socrates disagreed with and combated the Sophists. For him moral considerations were always important. His aim was to make good citizens.

## A character in Plato's dialogues

Socrates has left us no writings. We have two main sources for our knowledge of him. The first is the writer Xenophon, who was a man of conventional outlook and anxious to clear Socrates of the charge of corrupting the city's youth. Our other main source is Plato, a writer of genius and one of the first great builders of a philosophical system. Plato's work has come down to us in a series of dialogues. In these, two characters argue about philosophical questions. Socrates is nearly always one character in these dialogues. So it is hard to tell exactly when the text is telling us what Socrates taught and what specifically is the work of Plato. It is assumed that earlier dialogues reflect the teaching of Socrates, and that in later ones Plato has left his teacher behind and is embarking on his own original thought.

## Thought

Socrates held that virtue is the supreme good. No outside cause can deprive a person of virtue. He showed contempt for worldly goods. His concerns were mostly ethical. He always maintained he was ignorant; he was wiser than others only because he knew that he knew nothing. But he thought that the search for knowledge was more important than anything else and that only by achieving knowledge could one become virtuous. He sought knowledge by a method of question and answer (this is known as dialectic). He appears to have taught a doctrine of knowledge by reminiscence. According to this we learn by remembering what the immortal soul has learned in a life previous to our present existence.

Socrates tried to find out the real meaning of terms like 'good', 'just', 'true' and 'beautiful' by means of question and answer. He was fearless in exposing any reasoning that was inadequate. His relentless questioning of current assumptions did not always make him popular, but he was indifferent to that. Logic was at this time only in its infancy, but Socrates – whose logic was by no means perfect – could defeat anyone pitted against him in argument.

Socrates' central belief is that virtue is knowledge: correct action will follow from rational insight. All people desire good, therefore any evil they commit is due to ignorance of what is good. He himself claimed to know only that he knew nothing and thought his mission was not to pass on knowledge but to force all to examine their own opinions and presuppositions and discard those that could not be justified by reason.

## Socrates' death

In 399 BCE democracy had just been restored to Athens after a period of oligarchy following defeat in the war against Sparta. The leaders of this restored democracy brought Socrates to trial. No doubt the charges were politically motivated. Socrates had educated Alcibiades, who had been responsible for some of the recent political disasters. He had also educated Critias who was one of the most violent of the oligarchs. His accusers expected he would go into voluntary exile while awaiting trial. But he remained and defended himself. He was condemned to death by a majority of the jury. By custom Socrates had the right to propose an alternative penalty. The wisest course would have been to propose a hefty fine or exile. He proposed instead a ridiculously small fine. His execution was delayed for about a month in accordance with state religious practice. Socrates refused to avail himself of attempts arranged for him to escape. His last day on earth is described in Plato's dialogue *Phaedo*. He spent it discussing the immortality of the soul with his friends. He calmly drank the cup of hemlock which the jailer brought and then lay down. His last words

---

**Oligarchy** is a system of government where power is in the hands of a few individuals or of a few powerful families. An oligarch is a member of such a government.

**The Thirty** was a council of thirty oligarchs, a set of rulers imposed on Athens by Sparta after the Athenian defeat in the Peloponnesian war. They were famous for their despotism and numerous executions. They were deposed in 404–403 BCE and democracy was restored.

**Alcibiades** was an Athenian general of the democratic faction. He led his city in a disastrous adventure against Sicily. He was accused of sacrilege: mutilation of the Hermes (statues set up around the city to promote its power and fertility). He fled to the old enemy Sparta, but later returned to Athens. He died in exile, assassinated.

**Critias** was an Athenian politician and uncle of Plato. He was a member of the Thirty.

were: 'Crito, we owe a cock to Aesculapius; pay it, therefore, and do not neglect it.'

## Socrates' pursuit of truth

Socrates denied that he was wise; he had not discovered what virtue really consisted of, but he sought the cooperation of his listeners to get at the truth underlying confused opinions. He was inspired by a deep conviction that universally valid truth existed, that knowledge was the only basis of right action and that the good life consisted in knowing what was good and doing it. He was an example of intellectual thoroughness, devotion to truth and indifference to wealth and popularity.

## Appraisal

Socrates' interests involved ethical enquiry rather than scientific discovery.

The habit of general discussion (or dialectical method) can encourage logical reliability and precise definition. But it can also encourage nit-picking and excessive concentration on trivial exactness. It may in certain circumstances promote competition or opposition because people get locked into such roles. How likely do you think it is to bring about the discovery of new facts? What better ways might there be?

Socrates stressed the importance of definition (clarity in meaning) and was mainly occupied with seeking definitions of ethical terms, yet he rarely came to definite conclusions. Why was this? When you are arguing a moral point with someone, are you more interested in proving others wrong (and yourself right) than advancing knowledge or the argument?

It was Socrates' view that virtue is knowledge. Is this true? Is it possible to know what one should do, yet do something else? Should virtue also involve a determination to act correctly: even against one's own immediate interest?

## Three Platonic dialogues

In order to give a flavour of what and how the great man taught we give the shortest possible outline of three Platonic dialogues all featuring Socrates. They are all thought to be early dialogues. Early dialogues are likely to reflect Socrates' thought. Later dialogues are likely to involve what is distinctive about Plato's thought. (Note: these summaries are not an alternative to reading the real thing.)

---

### Meno

Meno asks Socrates how he can acquire virtue and Socrates discovers when he questions Meno that he does not understand the meaning of what he is talking about: Meno's definitions of virtue either use the word virtue to define virtue, or else just give examples or offer circular definitions.

How, asks Socrates, can one enquire about something if one does not know what one is enquiring about? Socrates suggests that our human souls are immortal and that between reincarnations we acquire knowledge of all things. Knowledge in this life is therefore an act of remembering what we learned in that other state. He concludes that virtue can be taught if virtue is knowledge. But there are no teachers of virtue, so virtue must be a gift from the gods.

---

### Gorgias

Socrates and Gorgias discuss rhetoric, the art of persuasive speech. Socrates holds that if the speaker has no knowledge of what he is talking about it is an example of the ignorant trying to teach the ignorant. If one talks about justice the speaker must have knowledge of justice. (Remember that rhetoric was used to argue cases in the courts, hence the interest in justice.) If one has knowledge of justice, one is just; therefore one cannot tolerate injustice. If one tolerated injustice one would be talking without having knowledge of what one was talking about. All people desire to act for the sake of some good; therefore people cannot act as they wish to act if they act in ignorance of the good. If we act wrongly we act in ignorance of the evil we do. It follows that punishment should aim at rehabilitation. It is better to be punished for one's misdeeds than to escape punishment.

Rhetoric, says Socrates, should be used to make people aware of injustice and of the cure for injustice.

Callicles suggests that justice is the rule of the stronger; Socrates suggests that the wise are the strong. Callicles argues that the wise seek pleasure for themselves. Socrates shows that pleasure and pain are not identical with the good and the bad.

---

## *Apology*

(Apology here means a defence of one's action, not a request to be excused.)

The oracle at Delphi had declared that Socrates was the wisest person of his day. Socrates says that if he is superior to others in wisdom it is only because he knows the extent of his ignorance. This dialogue is the record Plato leaves us of how Socrates defended himself against the charges for which he would in the end be executed. Socrates maintains that those who claimed to be wise and whose lack of wisdom he has exposed are in fact spreading false rumours about him in order to discredit him. He claims that it would be foolish of him to corrupt the people with whom he associated (the young), for corrupt and evil persons harm even those who have befriended them. Socrates points out that if he exposed weaknesses in the state then that did the state a service. He ought to be rewarded for being a gadfly to the state. Once he is condemned to death Socrates declares that one should not fear death for if death is annihilation it is not to be feared; on the other hand if it is a change to a better world then we will have the pleasure of the company of noble souls.

# Plato

Socrates tended to be critical rather than constructive in his philo-sophical production. Plato went beyond this. He was the first thinker to construct a great philosophical system.

## Life

Plato was born probably in 427 BCE, near Athens, into an aristocratic household. In his political thought he denounced democratic gov-ernment and was in favour of strong leadership to govern the 'ship of state'. This probably arose from his experience of living through pathetic and broken-down democratic government rather than from the prejudices of his aristocratic background. He is rumoured to have been a robust man and is likely to have fought in some of the later battles of the Peloponnesian war. He is said to have had an early taste for poetry, painting and tragedy but later came to distrust the arts.

Plato was a pupil of Socrates. He was due to go into politics, but the Athenian oligarchy embarked on a policy of repression and violence when Plato was a relatively young man. This may have dissuaded him. Certainly, the execution of his friend Socrates by the restored democ-racy made him distrust politicians even more. He attended Socrates' trial and endeavoured to get him to propose a hefty fine for himself, offering personally to stand security for it. He was absent from the death-scene through illness.

After Socrates' death Plato travelled, lived and discussed with other philosophers, eventually returning to Athens. In later life he travelled to Italy and Sicily. He appears to have got into trouble with the family of the tyrant of Syracuse and, as punishment, may have been sold as a slave. He was ransomed and returned to Athens, where he founded the Academy, the first European university.

Plato's aim was the education of statesmen and rulers. But his cur-riculum was broad, not just what might appear to be immediately useful. The Academy taught philosophy, mathematics, astronomy, the physical sciences and rhetoric. It encouraged the disinterested pursuit of knowledge for its own sake. His notion was that the ruler thus educated would not be a petty politician but rather a conviction politician fearlessly acting in accordance with eternal and changeless truths. Plato lectured in the Academy and his pupils took notes. These lectures were never published and have been lost. His dialogues, which have survived, were published and intended for popular reading. His most famous pupil was Aristotle, who came to study at the Academy in 367 BCE.

Plato made two more trips to Syracuse. He had hoped to play a part in the education of the new tyrant of Syracuse, but his dream of helping in the education of a 'philosopher-king' was never realized. Plato died in Athens in 347 BCE. It is thought that he did not marry.

---

**Timeline**

(All dates are BCE.)

427  Birth of Plato

422  Production of *The Wasps* by Aristophanes

407  Plato becomes a student of Socrates

406  Plato sees military service

404  End of the Peloponnesian war

400  Hippocrates writing his medical treatises

399  Death of Socrates

399  Plato travels abroad

395  More military service

388  Plato in Italy and Sicily

387  Plato founds the Academy

367  Aristotle enters the Academy

367  Further visits to Syracuse

347  Death of Plato

## Thought

### Reaction to the death of Socrates

Plato's great contributions to philosophy were in the areas of metaphysics, epistemology and political thought. In all of the above Socrates' influence was strong. Plato had a deep distrust of the notion of democracy. This is because he was profoundly shocked by the way the democratic faction had put Socrates to death. (We would be more inclined to use the word demagogy to describe the system to which Plato objected.)

---

**Metaphysics** is the study of being as being; speculation about the meaning of what is; the study of first principles and first causes; the rational knowledge of those realities that go beyond us; the rational study of things in themselves.

**Epistemology** is the branch of philosophy that studies the history, the methods and the principles of knowledge.

**Demagogy** is practised by politicians who play on the aspirations and prejudices of the greatest number to gain popularity and power: it suggests immediate majority or even mob rule.

**Democracy** is the rule of the people. In modern democracies majority rule is tempered by important principles such as respect for individuals, minority rights, liberty involving rights and duties, equality, the impartial administration of justice, rational discussion at all levels, the rule of law, deliberative and representative legislative assemblies, constitutionalism: limits to government action.

---

### Change and permanence

Plato was deeply influenced by the search for something permanent, eternal, permitting things to be known in themselves. All around he saw flux and change.

The writer Heraclitus (c. 550–c. 480 BCE) saw everything as change:

'You cannot step into the same river twice.' Only the ever-living fire was permanent.

Parmenides (c. 540–c. 480 BCE) declared the senses to be deceptive. The only true being was 'the One'. The whole of it is present everywhere. Whatever can be thought must exist because there is no thought without an object. If it can be thought it must exist at all times. Therefore there can be no change. For him there is no becoming or passing away.

I have a scar on my knee because I fell when I was a small boy. The cells in my body have changed many times since then, yet the scar remains. Why? Plato sought to reconcile the perception of change with the evidence of permanence.

## *The allegory of the cave*

Plato believed that we only come to know things if we think deeply about them and struggle with them. This is not an easy task and cannot be mastered in a short time. He wanted to show us that the reality of things is beyond our immediate grasp, but that most humans are content to accept the way things appear at first sight. For Plato this was not enough. He aimed to show the difference between the careless acceptance of appearance, which is the way of the ordinary person, and the deep enquiry into reality, which is the way of the philosopher. Plato told a story. It is sometimes referred to as the 'noble lie'. This means it is not literally true, but that it points to the way things are. It is the allegory of the cave.

Most people, says Plato, are like people sitting in a cave. They are looking at the back wall of the cavern. Just behind them is a low wall. Objects pass along this wall. Behind the low wall there is a fire. What do the people sitting facing the wall of the cave see? They see the shadows of those objects that the fire throws onto the back wall of the cavern. But this is not the way things really are. To see the way things really are one would have to come out into the sunlight. But do we want to come out into the sunlight? Most people are content to stay in the cave; they would be too frightened of reality to come out. They are comfortable with the way things appear to them. They are content with appearances. They do not wish to see things as they really are. They do not wish to be blinded by the sun. Only philosophers who are willing to spend years wrestling with appearance and reality are like those who come out into the sun and see things as they really are, even if they are different to what they had first thought.

### How one knows

There were a number of important influences on Plato. He was influenced by some of the mystery religions of the Greek world. He had a profound respect for mathematics. (Mysticism and mathematics were thought to be connected at that time.) He believed that reality is eternal and timeless and that change is an illusion. He had gained from Socrates his interest in ethics and he also tried to find explanations of the world in terms of goals rather than of causes. The good can only be known through a combination of intellectual and moral discipline.

### The importance of the philosopher

These presuppositions led Plato to conclude that the best state will be unchanging and already as perfect as possible: goodness and reality are timeless. The best state's rulers will be those who understand the eternal good. Only those who have gone through this discipline can share in the government of the state. The education of rulers must be long, thorough and painstaking. It must include mathematics, without which no wisdom is possible. Wisdom is a general disposition which is earned slowly and makes one capable of governing wisely. Leisure is essential to wisdom. One cannot find the time to think if one has to earn a living.

## *The threefold division of the soul*

Plato believed that the human soul had three parts. There was a rational, reasoning part. Wisdom was its most apparent virtue. There was a spirited, energetic part. Courage was its special virtue. Then there was a desiring, appetitive part, the virtue of which was temperance and submission to control.

## *Plato's theory of ideas*

The middle part of Plato's great work the *Republic* is occupied by philosophical considerations. Here is Plato's central contention that not until philosophers are kings will the state be untroubled. The *Republic* is a later work and is considered to be typical of Plato's ideas, even though Socrates is the chief speaker.

The philosopher is defined here as 'one who lives to see the truth'. He does not love beautiful things, good things or just actions; rather he loves absolute beauty, absolute goodness and absolute justice. The person who loves beautiful things, good things and just actions has only opinion, not knowledge. Opinion is of what is and of what is not, and so can be mistaken. Opinion is of particulars, intermediary between being and not-being. Opinion is concerned with the world of sense-objects. The philosopher, by contrast, has knowledge. Knowledge is of what is and cannot be mistaken. Knowledge concerns the supersensible, eternal world.

Plato's theory of ideas, which is also called his theory of forms, is his own creation. It is a doctrine of the meaning of general class-names. The word 'table' means not the table I am now working at or the table in front of you, but 'table' in general. 'Table' stands for the true reality. The table in front of me, the table near you, are just particular instances of the 'idea' or 'form' of 'table'.

The philosopher's concern is with the 'form' or 'idea' of 'table'. Philosophers are not concerned with particular tables, dogs, states, etc. Philosophy is a vision of truth, intellectual but also motivated by a loving desire for what is best, purest and highest.

*The influence of Sparta on Plato*

Plato's ideal state was influenced by Sparta. Sparta had defeated Athens after a long war. People were impressed by the severe simplicity of its (apparently) successful system. Spartan citizens trained for war. The aim of the whole organization of the state was to breed a race of invincible fighters. Girls were given the same physical training as boys. They were a specialized population. Their slaves cultivated the land and produced food. (They were another specialized population.) Land was divided equally among citizens; differences of riches and poverty were kept to a minimum. Meals were eaten in common. Stress was laid on the education of children. A high birth-rate was encouraged. Children belonged to the community rather than to their parents.

## The *Republic*

In the *Republic* Plato lays out the details of his ideal state. Socrates (Plato's philosopher and mouthpiece) has set out to show that justice is superior to injustice and is worthwhile for its own sake rather than because of its consequences. Socrates holds that justice is most visible at the level of the state rather than at the level of the individual. So he sets out to describe the ideal state where justice would be the ruling code.

There would be three classes of citizens: guardians, soldiers and workers. Guardians (men and women treated equally) would be those in whom reason was predominant. They would rule the state, but only after a long period of mental and physical training. Plato concentrates on the training of guardians in this work. They would live communally, free from the distractions of property and the temptations caused by the accumulation of wealth. After an initial period of training each yearly intake would specialize, becoming either rulers or soldiers. Soldiers were drawn from those in whom the spirited element was uppermost. They would develop their courage and train to guard the state. The principal virtues of workers would be those of the desiring, appetitive soul. They would attend to producing the wealth and food of the state. It was a state of strict division of labour. Justice was done as each class carried out its specialized duties and function, the duties and function for which it was, by training and aptitude, best fitted. Movement between classes was provided for.

The state must be involved in education. Only what is true and good must be taught. Poets use beautiful language and images, which are not literally true and even tell unethical tales. The simple are liable to be taken in by their subtle, dangerous poison. So Plato banished poets from his ideal state.

Marriages between men and women were to be arranged by lot from time to time. But in fact the lots were to be rigged so that the best breeders would come together and improve the genetic stock and health of the citizen body. Children would be taken from their parents at birth, raised communally and not know who their parents were. This was so that the welfare of the state rather than individual welfare would be uppermost.

## The *Symposium*

This work is concerned with the highest forms of love. Did you ever wonder why platonic love is so called? It is the form of love advocated by Plato in the *Symposium*. (A symposium in Greek was a banquet. Because people made a number of speeches discussing learned matters at this banquet, the word symposium has, in modern English, come to mean a meeting for learned purposes.)

Phaedrus claims that love between virtuous men and younger men is of the highest sort and the chief impulse to a noble life.

Pausanias makes a distinction between carnal love on the one hand and, on the other, the love of virtue and philosophy which is heavenly love.

Eryximachus claims that love is the rule of harmony which reconciles opposed elements in the body.

> Aristophanes, who is poking fun at the serious discussion, claims the body was originally round with four arms and ears, two faces, etc. The gods, to punish us, split them in two and ever since the halves have sought each other out to be reunited in love.
>
> Agathon says Love is the youngest and most beautiful of the gods, endowed with all virtues.
>
> Socrates claims that starting with a love of physical beauty one passes to know the ideal spirit of beauty itself. In this way one comes to share Love's divinity.

## Appraisal

With Plato we see philosophy take its most confident step away from earlier religious and mythological habits of thought. Yet at the same time it never completely leaves those ways of thinking behind. Plato is never reductionist, never paring down what he allows to be called knowledge. He always leaves an opening for human transcendence, our effort to surpass what is already obvious, known or achieved. Is this a strength or a weakness?

His concern for knowledge of what is true rather than of what is apparent led him to suggest that there is a real world to which only initiates have access. Is there any other evidence for this real world behind the apparent world, other than the way Plato allows it to follow from his definition?

His division of the soul into types and the general population into classes based on aptitude for various functions is rigid, lacks subtlety and does not allow for diversity and richness in a person's habits, interests and outlook. Athletes may appreciate the arts; philosophers have appetites.

His theory of the forms could more acceptably be proposed as a theory of logical classes (a matter of logic and language) rather than as a metaphysical theory.

Plato's theory of the forms is an effort to explain how we experience both change and permanence; we experience change through our senses and, by means of the mind, seek to understand continuing identity in the midst of change. Try to note other approaches to this question as you read on and reflect.

When we try to use abstract ideas and talk in terms of absolute truth, beauty or justice do we unconsciously echo Plato's theory of the forms?

Plato's distrust of democracy was based on the weaknesses he observed in the way it was practised in his day; he was not concerned to see how it might be improved. This is in line with his way of using language: justice can have nothing to do with injustice. It remains an empirical fact that polite people may, on occasion, be impolite; efficient people show instances of inefficiency, etc. His concern for effective general definitions caused him to distrust any use of language that could not be rigidly pigeonholed.

Plato's admiration for Sparta (and its recent success) caused him to be blind to the many improprieties in the daily application of its constitution.

The notion that justice was a matter of the harmonious functioning of the specialized classes appears strange to us. Nevertheless in ancient Greek times the determining ethical institution was the state. In the Middle Ages in Western Europe the determining ethical institution was the Church. One of the marks of modernity is that the determining ethical institution has become the individual. Is this a gain or a loss: what have we gained, what have we lost?

# 2 Aristotle: the Spirit of Rational Enquiry

Aristotle has dominated the intellectual landscape of Western Europe for about a thousand years. His work was once regarded with unquestioning reverence. When Galileo (1564–1642 CE) taught that the earth went around the sun, he was condemned for heresy. Why? Not because he contradicted the Bible, but because he had dared to contradict Aristotle! So who was this man regarded with such awe? Aristotle taught and wrote in Athens. He was a man of enormous intellectual energy, interested in everything. He comes across without the mystical quality of his great predecessor, Plato. His writings are more systematic. His style is more sober. He wrote, said a modern commentator, like a professor. (Did your school essays have an introduction, three sections and a conclusion? Blame Aristotle!)

Aristotle

## Life

Aristotle was born in 384 BCE in Stageira in the northeastern part of ancient Greece. His father was a doctor. He went to Athens at the age of 17 and enrolled in Plato's Academy. This was when the mystical, religious dimension of philosophy was occupying the Master's mind. Aristotle seems to have been more interested in observation and description, what we would now call the empirical sciences. Though he was eventually to differ from Plato in many ways, there is no evidence to suggest that he was hostile or ungrateful to his mentor. On the contrary, he professed the warmest admiration for him.

After the death of Plato, Aristotle left the Academy and lived for a while in Assos in northwestern Asia Minor, possibly setting up a local branch of the Academy. Here he married Pythias, the niece of the local ruler. There was a scandal that she was also this ruler's mistress, but, since this ruler appears to have been a eunuch, the story is unlikely. They later moved to Lesbos, an island off the coast of modern Turkey.

Aristotle was soon invited to the capital of Philip of Macedon, in the mountainous region to the north of Greece. His task was to undertake the education of the 13-year-old Macedonian prince, who was later to become Alexander the Great. Aristotle held the post of royal tutor for four years. His experiences, however, never led him to adopt a high view of empire. For Aristotle, the ideal political unit remained the Greek city-state.

In 335 BCE Aristotle returned to Athens and opened his own school, the Lyceum, just outside the city. It was apparently named after the nearby temple of Apollo Lukeios. Lectures were held there, but it also became a centre for established scholars and thinkers, and built up a fine library. Members of the Lyceum apparently often held their discussions walking up and down, sheltered from the sun by a colonnade or shady passage. Aristotelian thought is frequently referred to as 'peripatetic', from this habit of walking up and down whilst learning, discussing and thinking. It was during this period that he wrote most of his books. The Lyceum was much more a centre for research and the collection of data than the semi-religious and mystical Academy of Plato.

Alexander the Great died in 323 BCE, and there was a strong reaction against Macedonian control throughout Greece. Aristotle suffered by association from this resentment and wisely withdrew from Athens. He died of an illness in 322 BCE. He was 62.

---

## Timeline

(All dates are BCE.)

431–404  Peloponnesian war between Athens and Sparta

400  Hippocrates' medical writings

384  Birth of Aristotle

367  Aristotle enters the Academy

359  Philip II becomes King of Macedon

350  Building of the theatre of Epidaurus in Greece

347  Death of Plato

After 347  BCE Aristotle teaches away from Athens

345  approx. Marriage of Aristotle

343–339  Aristotle tutor to Alexander the Great

341  Birth of Epicurus

335  Birth of Zeno

335  Aristotle opens the Lyceum

334–323  Great expedition of Alexander the Great to Persia, Egypt
                 and India

323  Death of Alexander the Great

322  Death of Aristotle

321  Break-up of Alexander's empire

300  Euclid's *Elements*

## Thought

### Physics and metaphysics

Not everybody was satisfied with Plato's doctrine of the forms. It was a doubling of visible things. One of its purposes was to explain why there were many things in the world. It did not help to suppose the existence of a parallel host of forms. If things exist by virtue of the forms, it does not explain coming-to-be and passing away. Often, when Plato tried to explain how the forms related to the things of which they were forms, his language was simply poetic figure of speech.

Aristotle set out to tackle this weakness in Plato's teaching with his theory of universals.

---

**Physics** is the study of nature. It comes from the Greek word *'phusis'*, meaning nature. But it is nature as a process of growth or becoming.

**Metaphysics** is the study of being as being; speculation about the meaning of what is; the study of first principles and first causes; the rational knowledge of those realities that go beyond us; the rational study of things in themselves.

---

### Universals

Some words signify things that are unique: the 'Taj Mahal' or 'Jack the Ripper'. Other words signify things that are common to many instances: 'bed', 'chair', 'dog', 'black', 'sweet'. Universals refer to these later words. Aristotle made a distinction between a substance and a universal. A substance is what is meant by a proper name. A universal is what is meant by a class-name or an adjective. It indicates *the sort of thing* something is; it does not indicate a particular thing. It is what a number of particular things have in common. The chair I am sitting on at my desk, the chair beside my bed and the chair out in the garden all look different and are made of different materials. What they have in common, making them recognizable as chairs, is referred to as a universal. Nowadays we would be inclined to say that this similarity has to do with language rather than with the analysis of reality or with metaphysics.

### Essence

This is another term used by Aristotelian philosophers. It is not the same as universal. An 'essence' is what an item or event is by its nature. It cannot lose that nature without ceasing to be itself. Essence comes before existence.

### Form and matter

If I take a piece of children's play-dough and roll it into a ball, the matter is play-dough. The form is the ball-like shape I have given it. Form gives matter its substance.

Aristotle says the soul is the form of the body. Soul is what makes each body what it is and gives it its purpose. Aristotle says the form of a thing is its essence and primary substance. Forms are substantial; universals are not. The form and matter of a thing both exist before a thing is made.

Matter without form is only a potentiality. The more form a thing has the more actuality it has. These notions of 'potentiality' and 'actuality' are very important to Aristotle for explaining change.

There is a hierarchy of existence. An unhewn stone is in a state of potentiality with regard to a hewn stone. This hewn stone is in a state of actuality with regard to the unhewn stone, but it is in a state of potentiality with regard to a house. To understand how Aristotle explains change we must first look at his notion of cause.

### Cause

Aristotle wished to give a classification of the notion of cause. He divided his analysis into four main types of cause:

(1) *Material cause* is the matter that goes to make up an object, the sounds that go to make up a word, the pieces of evidence that go to make up a logical conclusion.

(2) *Formal cause* is the form that is necessary so that the object may be as it is. A ball may need rubber as its material cause, but it needs roundness as its formal cause. A game needs a set of rules as its formal cause.

(3) *Efficient cause* is what starts off an event or a process. The advice one receives may be the efficient cause of deciding to be an engineer. The inspiration one received from a teacher may be the efficient cause of an interest in poetry. Flinging a cigarette-end out through a car window may be the efficient cause of a forest fire.

(4) *Final cause* is the aim or goal which one sets out to achieve. The final cause of this afternoon's training session is the winning of next weekend's match.

## Teleology

We think of cause as something that happens *before* something else happened. The cause of the fire was the match being struck and applied. Aristotle often considered the final cause as the most important. The cause of the fire was the fact that the cold person wanted to get warm. In this case the cause (the warming up) came *after* the event. Cause is seen in terms of the goal of a fire. This is what is meant by teleology. We think of nature as being rather like a machine, which is why we think in terms of efficient cause. Aristotle thought of nature as being rather like an artist, struggling to realize an idea.

We can now understand how Aristotle explained change using the notions of form, matter and cause.

There are two basic elements in every natural happening: firstly an element which remains the same (even if it is subject to variations) and secondly, genuine change of properties.

Matter can be given various forms. The form of an item or event at a given moment is its actuality, what it has become at that moment: for example a seed. But a seed has potentiality. Every item or event can only be understood using both its matter and its form: how it moves or alters, replacing one form with another. The seed becomes a flower. Each item or event is always in some state and is in the process of changing into another state. It has a changing side, 'form' and an unchanging side, 'matter'.

Aristotle's thoughts on these subjects are found in the *Physics* and in the *Metaphysics*. He contributed the word 'metaphysics' to human language. They are his thoughts on such things as go 'beyond what is physical'. The text of the *Metaphysics* was also bound in a volume 'after the *Physics*'. Both meanings are suggested as the origin of the word.

## Logic

Aristotle's work on logic is now out of date, yet in its day it was admirable. Aristotle became an 'authority' and no one was allowed to question his say-so. It is not a philosophical way of thinking, yet it is what happened. After Aristotle there was virtually no development in logic for 2,000 years. Aristotle was mainly interested in deductive reasoning. Here one argues from general established facts to a particular case or to another general case. To do this he used the syllogism. In this type of reasoning if the evidence is true and the manner of arguing valid then the conclusion must be true.

The first editors of Aristotle's writings on this subject classified his work on logic under the heading *Organon*, which means 'tool' or 'instrument'. He himself did not consider it to be a body of knowledge but a process. He wanted to arrive at a process or procedure which could be shown to work regardless of the content.

## Deductive reasoning

We now turn to some more technical terms:

*Propositions* are sentences that take the form of subject and predicate: 'The dog is excited.' The subject is what we are talking about: 'the dog'. The predicate is what we say about it: 'is excited'. Propositions must take the form: the members of one class are (or are not) members of another class. This member of the class of 'dogs' is also a member of the class of 'excited beings'.

There are four types of proposition, e.g.:

All men are mortal.
Some men are mortal.
Some men are not mortal.
No men are mortal.

Propositions are either true or false.

---

**Inferences** are the reasoning processes we use to draw conclusions based on the evidence presented to us. We can reason wrongly, in which case the inference is invalid, or we can reason correctly and the inference is valid.

---

Remember: propositions are true or false. Inferences are valid or invalid.

### The syllogism

This is the form of reasoning favoured by Aristotle:

A syllogism is a group of three propositions.
There are two premises.
A premise is a proposition put forward as evidence.
From these two premises a conclusion is drawn.

Here is an example of a syllogism:

All submarines are underwater craft.
No pleasure vessels are underwater craft.
Therefore no submarines are pleasure vessels.

To arrive at a true conclusion, both the premises must be true and also the inference must be valid.

## Inductive reasoning

But how does one reach universally true propositions in the first place? There is another type of reasoning called inductive reasoning. This tries to arrive at general, true propositions on the basis of observation. It works a bit like this:

Socrates is a man and is mortal,
Plato is a man and is mortal,
Aristotle is a man and is mortal . . .
Therefore all men are (probably) mortal.

Inductive reasoning tends to produce probable conclusions. From these probable conclusions other conclusions may be deduced and tested against reality. Aristotle did not develop inductive reasoning. We had to wait until the work of Francis Bacon (1561–1626 CE) and John Stuart Mill (1806–73 CE) for developments in this field.

Nowadays, Aristotelian logic is outdated and not widely taught. If you want to learn logic today you must learn symbolic logic which uses mathematical notation. Aristotle's work on logic is found in his book, the *Prior Analytics*.

## Aesthetics

Aristotle's aesthetics, his teaching about beauty, are contained in the *Poetics*; we only possess about half the text.

Poetry, he teaches, is the imitation of human life in its universal aspects. Comedy is the imitation of what is ugly. (We laugh when we see something deformed.) Tragedy is the imitation of serious action aiming at purging the emotions (catharsis) by means of pity and fear.

The tragic hero is one who brings about his own downfall through a flaw in his own character, yet he is nobler than most and thus a hero.

The three most important moments in a tragedy are the reversal of fortune, the discovery of the important factor which brings about the dénouement and the suffering of the hero.

Aristotle's teaching about comedy has been lost.

## *The soul*

Aristotle taught that there are three kinds of substances. First, there are sensible and perishable substances, e.g., animals and plants. Second, there are sensible objects which do not perish, e.g., the stars and planets; they move but that is the only change that can be observed in them. Third, there are substances that are neither sensible nor perishable: God and the rational soul in a human being.

We are not sure if Aristotle taught that the soul is immortal: his writings are a little unclear. In his book *De Anima* he pokes fun at the notion of the transmigration of souls and sees the soul as very much bound up with the body. Body is the matter of human beings, soul their form. Soul is the essence of the body, the actuality of the body and the final cause of the body. Yet mind is higher than the body, it is the speculative part of the soul. In the *Nicomachean Ethics* Aristotle talks of the soul as having a rational and irrational part. Reason is divine, so life in accordance with reason is divine. As we live such a life we make ourselves immortal. This is not an individual immortality; it is a share in God's immortality. Individual identity is connected with the body and the irrational part of the soul.

Aristotle's thoughts on the immortality of the soul resonate with the modern reader, yet are in some ways unfamiliar. Christianity took many early Greek ideas and moulded them into a Christian outlook. It is fair to say that without Socrates, Plato and Aristotle, Christian theology would have developed quite differently from the way that it did. Later Christian thinkers depended heavily on Greek modes of thought to construct the Christian outlook and worldview. They ultimately went on to raise the huge edifice of Christian civilization that is the inheritance of modern Europe and America, and elsewhere. Out of this legacy also came the scientific mindset, the secular tradition and vindication of human rights which are the cultural context of contemporary Western peoples.

Aristotle also developed arguments to prove the existence of God, but as these were later developed and brought to a more refined form by the great medieval philosopher Thomas Aquinas, we shall wait until we come to him before looking at what are known as the theistic arguments.

## Aristotle's ethics: the golden mean

Aristotle laid out his teaching on ethics, the study of the principles governing what is right and wrong, in his book the *Nicomachean Ethics*. He based his teaching on happiness. What is the good life for a person? It is a life of happiness. 'Happiness is an activity of the soul in accord with perfect virtue.' Happiness is an activity. It is not a goal. It accompanies activities. It is a way of being caught up in the diverse activities of life. So how ought we to behave? We ought to behave so as to achieve happiness.

This brings us to one of Aristotle's most famous doctrines: the doctrine of the golden mean. ('Mean' here means a comfortable balance.) If I go out for the evening, how much should I drink? Achieve a comfortable balance, Aristotle would say, between drinking too little and drinking too much. If I go to a party how should I behave? Achieve a comfortable balance between being too shy and retiring and being too boisterous.

In this way there are different correct ways of behaviour for different people. What is good for one may not suit another. The golden mean requires, perhaps, a degree of trial and error. Act moderately. Seek the mean between two extremes. Each of the extremes is a vice.

Courage is the mean between cowardice and rashness. The virtue of generosity is the mean between the vices of prodigality and meanness. Excess should not be calculated mathematically. It is apparent to the person of practical wisdom.

You can see that much of Aristotle's doctrine of the mean uses wordplay. It is quite possible, and amusing, to play a game and engineer ridiculous examples of the golden mean: 'Correct action is a mean between right and wrong.' 'The virtuous person practises mediocrity as a mean between stupidity and intelligence.' It is not a ready-made simple rule.

Aristotelian ethics typify the common-sense outlook of prudent persons who recognize their worth and expect others to recognize it also, who have leisure and cultivation and give service to the society in which they live. Today there is renewed interest in Aristotle's ethical teaching as societies become more diverse and composed of people from many different backgrounds who seek to work out new ways of living together in harmony and mutual respect. It involves coming to terms with conflicting, even contradictory, demands and achieving balance and harmony.

## Other ethical standards

Aristotle's ethics are *teleological*, that is to say they concentrate on goals or targets. There are other standards that have to be taken into account. One has to judge that an action or proposal is just and good *in itself*. The action proposed must have a *good and just cause*, it must be proposed with *a right intention*. The action must have *good consequences* and possible consequences, other than the ones proposed, must be taken into account.

## Politics

Aristotle's thoughts on politics concentrate on the city-state that was the common political unit in his time. He was both older and outlived Alexander the Great, yet there is no mention of his fearless and brash experiment. His thoughts on affairs of state are found in his work the *Politics*. Aristotle had little interest in the mechanics of government. He held the state to be the highest political and ethical organism. It took ethical priority over both the family and the individual. Individuals cannot fulfil their purpose unless they are part of the state.

The state is composed of families. Slaves are part of a family, and it is right to make slaves of prisoners of war. The naturally inferior are better off when ruled by their superiors. Aristotle disapproves of trade: things are made for use and the natural way to acquire wealth is the skilful management of land.

Aristotle criticizes the communism of Plato's ideal state. The abolition of the family is objectionable as family and private property are the fundamentals of the state. Communal ownership of wives would mean there would be no one to manage the household. Without private property the virtue of benevolence would disappear.

To prevent revolution three things are needed. The first is government propaganda in education. The second is respect for law and justice in administration – they are intrinsic parts of good government. Rule in accord with law means the government of willing citizens. Third, states should be large enough to have economic independence and small enough for the citizens to know each other.

Citizens should be educated in what is useful to them, but the purpose of education is virtue. By the word 'virtue' the Greeks meant 'human excellence'. Aristotle restricts citizenship to landowning citizens who are freed (by the institution of slavery) from the toil of working the land and who are highly educated. Thus they have the culture, leisure and virtue to exercise responsible and virtuous government.

## The classification of constitutions

Aristotle gave a famous classification of state constitutions. He drew up what we would now call a database of 158 constitutions of states in his day. All have disappeared except for the constitution of Athens. Furthermore, he classified constitutions into six types. To do this he first of all made two sorts of judgement.

In the first judgement Aristotle distinguished between true and perverted states. There are true states whose aim is virtue. These states seek the good of the great mass of the citizens. Then there are perverted states. They aim at power or wealth or the well-being of one powerful class to the disadvantage of all others. The next judgement is threefold. Aristotle distinguished between states where power was in the hands of one person, in the hands of just a few powerful individuals or families, or in the hands on many citizens. He then combined the two types of judgement:

|  | **True states** | **Perverted states** |
| --- | --- | --- |
| *Power exercised by one* | Monarchy | Tyranny |
| *Power exercised by a few* | Aristocracy | Oligarchy |
| *Power exercised by many* | Polity | Democracy |

Aristotle recognized that there are two claims to power: the rights of property and the welfare of the greatest number. Wealth has no absolute claim to power, but it does have consequences: leisure, breeding and education. The number of people affected by decisions is important and a steady, restrained and serious public opinion is necessary.

Aristotle considered virtuous monarchy as probably the best form of government. If a virtuous king can be found he would be 'a god amongst men'. He spent some time discussing each of the different types of constitution.

We may be surprised to note that Aristotle considered democracy to be a perverted form of government, but we must remember that when he used the word 'polity' he meant something like what we would call democracy; when he used the word 'democracy' he meant something like demagogy or mob-rule.

Democracy nowadays involves a number of elements unknown in Aristotle's day. These include an insistence on individual human rights, the independence of the courts, the independent and universal application of law without fear or favour, the protection of minorities, representative assemblies supported by the authority of the electorate to debate public policy and be involved in long-term planning, executive bodies to carry out such policy; all such bodies being independent of the fickle whim of an easily changed popular mood.

## Appraisal

In philosophical terms of rational argument Aristotle is an improvement on Plato. He is without his teacher's mystical element. (Would you agree that this is an improvement? Try to note other thinkers who insist on a mystical element in their apprehension of what it is to be human.) Moreover, Aristotle's writings are more systematic and sober, without the drama and distraction of the dialogue form.

Much of Aristotle's physics and metaphysics may seem strange to us today, accustomed as we are to a different way of analysing matter, yet his was the first attempt to provide a totally critical and objective vocabulary for such a task.

In his physics, metaphysics, logic and ethics Aristotle foreshadowed what was to be the task of analytical philosophers of the twentieth century CE: to provide a critique of language. This prevents us from being fooled by the structure of language into imagining problems that do not exist.

Aristotle's logic is now seen as inadequate, yet he was the first to systematize laws of thought. His analysis of cause was most important. The notion of efficient cause is still used in modern science. Read any detective novel and you will see how important is the analysis of cause. Biologists and evolutionists still use the notion of teleology or final cause, and this is an important working tool. The doubt that David Hume (see Chapter 8) has cast over the whole notion of causation is extremely worrying to many modern scientists.

Aristotle held that the highest activity of the soul is speculation. What is your view of this? What other activity of the soul might you consider to be of higher value? Aristotle's notions of the soul are strange to us and have been changed considerably by Christian theology and modern psychology. But the vocabulary still comes in part from Aristotle.

One of the most pervasive doctrines of modern ethics is utilitarianism. Thank Aristotle for the stress that both the notion of happiness and the importance of the greater number receive in that school of thought.

Aristotle's ethics are receiving renewed attention in the late twentieth and early twenty-first centuries. This is because modern thinkers frequently distrust 'grand narratives', overarching, all-explaining doctrines and prefer a 'case-by-case' approach to moral decision-making. Aristotle's ethical thought is seen to be 'non-essentialist' and thus helpful.

Many of Aristotle's political concerns are out of date, and the vocabulary used by the ancient Greeks has changed considerably and acquired a different meaning today. Yet in Aristotle's concern with the small city-state one can see many parallels with modern local democracy. The importance of communities taking responsibility for the well-being of their immediate area, the 'principle of subsidiarity' that is supposed to be a feature of the modern European Union, would be of interest to Aristotle, and reading his thoughts on similar issues can be instructive for us today.

Aristotle considered the cultivation of leisure to be a worthy activity, as it allowed time for contemplation and the exchange of ideas. It also afforded time for free citizens to be involved in the government of the state, in the administration of its justice system and in the defence of the state in times of war. What would you consider to be the highest value of leisure? Who should govern the state, defend it and administer its justice system, and how and by whom should they be supported?

If Aristotle's views are seen as having held sway for too long, that is not his fault. It is because later thinkers refused to follow the critical path that he took, and so fell into what Kant (see Chapter 9) was to call 'dogmatic slumbers'.

*After Aristotle*

Aristotle's influence was enormous. His Lyceum survived until the adoption of Christianity by the Roman empire. Shortly after this it was shut down as a centre of pagan teaching. The works of Plato continued to be fairly well known and were adapted as the theoretical basis for Christian thought, which was then beginning to develop. Many of the works of Aristotle, in particular his logical writings, were lost, and in the early medieval universities thinkers struggled to solve problems he had already dealt with. His writings were, however, treasured and respected in the Arab world, where the great centres of learning in Baghdad were vital in preserving them. Aristotle's thought was virtually unknown in Christian Europe until contacts developed between scholars of the Christian West and those of Arabic nations. These contacts were often made through the great centres of Arab civilization in Spain.

The British philosopher Bertrand Russell (1872–1970) has noted that it is fashionable to view the Greeks with superstitious reverence. He felt, however, that the temper of their mind was abstract rather than scientific: they tended to reason deductively from what was self-evident rather than establish new facts by inductive reasoning. Nevertheless they invented geometry, without which modern science would have been impossible. They also invented nearly all the hypotheses that have dominated philosophy. Theirs was the blending of religion and reasoning, moral aspiration and logic.

# 3 Epicurus and Zeno: How to Lead a Good Life

Epicurus and Zeno are two examples of later Greek thought. Each started a trend in philosophy which was popular and lasted for many centuries. They both lived at roughly the same time. Epicurus was responsible for a line of thought that is still known as Epicureanism (sometimes called Hedonism), but he did not really teach what most people now mean by these words. In purely philosophical terms, later disciples wrought very little change in his thought. Zeno was responsible for what we call Stoicism. This, on the other hand, was very influential and had many versions and variations. Both thinkers are important for the development of ethics.

## Hedonism

Hedonism is the teaching that pleasure is the only good. Plato had denied that the good life had anything to do with pleasure. Aristotle felt that pleasure must make some contribution to happiness. Hedonists said there was no other good. However, Epicurean teachings deal mostly with how to live modestly but with pleasure. If you seek pleasure in an extreme way, you will without doubt cause pain: over-indulge in the pleasure of intoxicating drink and you will suffer the pain of a hangover. So just enjoy a modest drink and you will have pleasure without pain. Epicureanism is about living pleasantly and avoiding any disagreeable cost of such a lifestyle: it urges one to set out to avoid pain rather than seek pleasure if it will later produce pain.

## Stoicism

Stoicism was the most powerful ethical teaching in the ancient world before the rise of Christianity. It offers advice to individuals about how to come to personal salvation in a world descending into chaos and disintegration. Good and evil depend upon the self. Others may have power over you – they can impose torture, prison or slavery on you – but if you are indifferent to these external powers, outsiders will not have dominion over you. Virtue resides in the will; only the will is good or bad.

# Epicurus

### Life

Epicurus was born on Samos, a Greek island in the Aegean Sea, near the Turkish coast, in about 342 BCE. He went to Athens at the age of 18, where he did military service. He listened to a variety of teachers

Epicurus

in different Greek cities. In his mid-thirties he moved to Athens, where he opened his own school of philosophy.

This was an unusual school. Its premises appear to have been a walled garden, set apart from the bustle of the city. Epicurus willed it to his followers after his death. He seems to have been regarded with awe as a teacher during his lifetime. His teachings were delivered to his pupils to be learned off by heart. It was an act of betrayal to change or question what he wrote. For a philosopher, this is a serious failing.

We possess very few of Epicurus' writings. Even though one ancient author declares that he wrote over 300 books, only a few fragments remain. Our main source of what he taught is considered to be the Roman poet Lucretius (91–51 BCE). The contents of his poem had barely changed from the writings of the master, 300 years earlier. The main idea in this teaching is that human beings should be helped to acquire peace of soul and to be free from fear of death and of the gods.

Epicurus himself was, at the end of his life, in great pain, but bore his suffering cheerfully, being insistent to the end that the children of Metrodorus, one of his first disciples, should be looked after. This emphasizes a point about his school, which was less a school than a community where all shared friendship and all sorts and conditions of people might be pupils. The school/community included disciples, friends, their children – even slaves and courtesans. The lifestyle was very simple, and the food extremely plain, often just bread and water. Cheese was served when they decided they were really going to have a feast. (This diet may have been the consequence of the master's recurrent poor health). Epicurus died in 270 BCE. He never married.

For all that, and taking into account the detail of his philosophical thought which we will sketch below, Epicurus appears to us as an overcautious, unadventurous, fearful and rather self-centred individual. (One gets the impression that had he lived today he would have spent all his money on insurance policies and have enjoyed little.)

## Thought

### *Pleasure*

The main thrust of Epicurus' philosophy was directed towards tranquillity of mind. Pleasure was the supreme good. This included all the physical pleasures: taste, touch, hearing, sight, smell. The chief pleasure was the pleasure of the stomach. The pleasures of the mind came second. The chief pleasure of the mind was contemplating the pleasure of the body.

This attitude did have the advantage that one could contemplate pleasure without having to contemplate pain. Nevertheless, virtue meant prudence in the search for pleasure. Justice meant acting in such a way as not to fear other people's resentment – which is rather a restricted and ungenerous view.

### *Dynamic and static pleasure*

Early hedonists thought in terms of dynamic pleasure and static pleasure. Dynamic pleasures were when one set out to achieve a desired goal; the fact that one desires something is seen as a pain because one lacks something. Static pleasures were when one was in a state of balance: one no longer lacked or desired; the state one would wish to be in was present. A dynamic pleasure is drinking when one is thirsty; a static pleasure is not being thirsty.

Epicurus thought one was better off in a state of static pleasure: it is pure and one does not run the risks of pain that accompany being in a state of desire. Thus he would always aim at static pleasure, which does not depend upon the pain of lack of fulfilment. Epicurus always aimed for quiet pleasures, never for strong sensations. He strongly disapproved of sexual pleasure: it never does one good, and is often harmful.

### *The avoidance of pain*

The absence of pain, rather than the presence of pleasure, became the essence of Epicureanism. Wealth, honour and success were all futile; they made you restless when you could be contented. For Plato and Aristotle philosophy was the pursuit of knowledge and required rigorous intellectual disciplines such as mathematics and logic. For Epicurus it was a practical scheme requiring common sense.

Epicurus advised his disciples to flee from every form of culture. They should not get involved in public life. If you became successful and acquired power there was an increase in the number of those who envied or even wished to harm you.

Epicurus did, however, value friendship, and it appears that he frequently put himself out for his friends, even though if he strictly followed his own rules he would have been more selfish. He appears to have felt strongly for the suffering of the mass of humanity and wished they would seek consolation in his philosophy.

Above all, Epicurus wanted to avoid fear. For him the two great sources of fear were fear of the gods and fear of death. The Greeks had only very hazy notions of what happened after one died, and they did not want to learn more. They rarely portrayed the dead as happy. All the stories of heroes visiting the Underworld (Odysseus for example) and meeting those they knew in life portray the dead as unhappy. Religion, with few exceptions, appeared to encourage the view that the departed were unhappy. Religion for Epicurus was not a source of consolation but of terror. If one were immortal one would never be released from fear or pain.

### Epicurus' atomic theory

Epicurus was a materialist; he believed everything to be composed of matter. The world was made up of atoms and the void; falling through the void, atoms collided with each other and developed into objects. The soul also was material. At death the soul separated from the body, its atoms were dispersed. The gods existed, but were sensible hedonists applying themselves to their own pleasure (or lack of pain). They did not get involved in human affairs and they sensibly avoided public life. There was thus no reason why humans should fear them.

## Appraisal

The fundamental ideas of hedonism come from two sources. One is a psychological *description* of human actions: whatever human beings do they are always motivated by pleasure. So if an individual performs an act of self-sacrifice to save loved ones, that person is motivated by the pleasure of knowing that others are safe, better off or more contented. The second part of the doctrine is a *judgement* that one *ought* to seek pleasure; it is the only thing of decisive value.

---

### Intrinsic value and instrumental value

If I value something because I want it for itself, then I believe that whatever my goal is, it has *intrinsic* value. If I value something because it allows me to achieve something I want, then that object or activity has *instrumental* value. It is an instrument which allows me to achieve the goal beyond. If playing football is something I love, cherish and am passionate about, then football has *intrinsic* value. Togging out and training three times a week on winter nights is a means to playing at a high standard and with a good team. In this case training has *instrumental* value.

---

Hedonism has the advantage and elegance of putting forward a single reason for every type of conscious, intentional action human beings might take. This covers goals that are both intrinsically and instrumentally valuable. So all conscious human behaviour can be explained by one goal: pleasure is what all individuals aim for ultimately. Do you agree? If you were to list others, how long would your list be?

But is the pursuit of pleasure the ultimate aim of every human being? If a person studies hard to become a success in business we might say that success is what ultimately gives that person pleasure. But if that person also marries and has a family, must we then say that ultimately marriage and family are there for the sole purposes of pleasure, even (in some cases) of success in business. Is human motivation not a little more complex?

If we wish to hang on to the theory and say that success is one person's pleasure, money another's, sex a third's, then we no longer have a value-free, methodical *description* of human behaviour. We merely say that people desire what they desire. In addition it reduces ethical thinking to what each individual desires. But we think ethically because we are not alone on a desert island; we are not isolated individuals. We think ethically because we are in the presence of others. 'What ought I to do?' 'How will this impinge on others?' and 'What ought all the others around me to do?' – all these questions are linked.

So hedonism is more than a description. It is a value-judgement of what one *ought* to do. Hedonism says the good life consists of a life of pleasure and one ought to act so as to acquire pleasure. Epicurus said that some pleasures may be accompanied by pain. Smoking is a pleasure to which many are addicted. Is the addiction a pain? (They now cannot do without it.) What is more, one person's smoking can harm others. If smoking is my pleasure, we cannot say that the good life is a life of pleasure.

Often the life of pleasure cannot be separated from the pain that goes with it. In addition we all have *duties* as well as pleasures. These duties can be monotonous and irksome. Is it acceptable to neglect one's duty because one is thus avoiding pain? Have you ever suggested to the taxman that you should not be required to pay taxes due because you were avoiding the pain of paying out money or seeking pleasure by tax evasion? What do you think he might say and how might he justify himself ethically for his imposition?

The hedonism of Epicurus had a great-great-grandchild in the ethical teachings of Jeremy Bentham (1748–1832) and John Stuart Mill (1806–73). This was sometimes called ethical hedonism (better known as utilitarianism) and promoted the ethical doctrine of 'the greatest happiness of the greatest number'. In some versions it sought to judge actions on the standards of both the quantity and quality of pleasure and pain produced.

Can one really pursue happiness or pleasure? Modern psychology suggests that happiness is something that accompanies the pursuit of other goals. We strive for other things without thinking of pleasure or happiness. We discover later that we have been happy during these activities. But we were not concentrating on pleasure. The pleasure comes as a bonus which we did not consciously seek.

---

**Metaphysics** is the study of being as being; speculation about the meaning of what is; the study of first principles and first causes; the rational knowledge of those realities that go beyond us; the rational study of things in themselves.

**Logic** is the study of the procedures which produce correct, methodical and internally coherent reasoning.

**Materialism** is a philosophical doctrine claiming that nothing exists except matter and that all thought, feeling, mind or will may be explained in terms of that physical reality.

**Ethics** is the study of the principles governing what is right and wrong. It is concerned with notions such as 'good', 'obligation' and 'duty'.

---

### Timeline

(All dates are BCE.)

350  Heraclides of Pontus suggests the earth rotates on its own axis

342  Birth of Epicurus

336  Birth of Zeno

332  Alexander the Great beats Darius III at the battle of Issus

324  Epicurus arrives in Athens

321  Empire of Alexander the Great is divided amongst his companions

316  Zeno arrives in Athens

307  Epicurus opens his school in Athens

300  Zeno founds his school in Athens

299  Old Testament book of *Ecclesiastes*

285  Building of the first great lighthouse at Pharos

270  Death of Epicurus
269  Minting of first Roman silver coins
264  Death of Zeno
264  First Punic war between Rome and Carthage
250  Archimedes propounds theory of the lever; Eratosthenes
        measures the circumference of the earth; Aristarchus of
        Samos suggests that the earth moves round the sun

# Zeno

## Life

Zeno was the founder of the stoic school. He was born on Cyprus, possibly in 336 BCE. He is believed to have been Phoenician. He died in Athens in 264 BCE. His father ran a trading business, and Zeno seems to have worked with him for a while. He arrived in Athens at about the age of 20. He read Xenophon's and Plato's accounts of Socrates and was smitten by their memories of the man. In particular he admired Socrates' fortitude when on trial, his calmness when he was unjustly condemned to death, his scorn of luxury and indifference to creature comforts.

Zeno was also attracted by the Cynics but he listened to many teachers of philosophy in Athens and eventually, at about the age of 35, founded his own school. Only a very few fragments of his written work remain. The name stoic comes from the Greek word *stoa*, meaning a porch. Zeno taught his followers in Athens under a shaded colonnade called *stoa poikile*, or painted porch. Stoicism had a long and varied history and transplanted to Rome with great ease.

We know little of his private life, but he may have committed suicide.

## Thought

Unlike Epicureanism there were many variations and developments in stoic teaching and its orthodoxy was not rigidly controlled. There is little room here to discuss these developments and we must be content with an outline of the teachings of Zeno.

### Materialism

Zeno did not go in for metaphysical abstractions. He was a materialist. He never doubted the evidence of the senses. The real world was solid and material, so were God and virtue and justice: all solid and material. This seems odd. We may just conclude that Zeno was a materialist and any attempts by subtle minds to trip him up were given that sort of reply. These things were not, for him, important.

Stoic physics are not now important, but they give an insight into how the ancients thought. Originally there was only one element: fire, then the others (air, water, earth) came into being. Zeno taught a form of cosmic determinism: everything is strictly controlled by rigid laws; everything that has happened will happen again and the cycle will go round once more, and then again endlessly.

Stoic philosophy was not about metaphysical speculation or about theory of knowledge; it too was advice to individuals as to how they should live a good life. Stoic metaphysics and logic were, of course, to change, but stoic ethics remained quite stable throughout its long history.

### Stoic virtue

Stoic philosophy, like that of Epicurus, was offered to individuals in a disintegrating world. That is to say, the old certainties of the Greek world were passing away; power was shifting and being employed in new ways. The days of the city-state, where each individual fitted into a small social unit with people having a sense of local identity, were at an end, to be replaced by vast empires. Alexander the Great's was the first in the West (there had of course been earlier vast empires further east). Stoicism taught its disciples to learn to be indifferent to outside influences.

Everything is controlled by a kindly providence overseeing all, and everything has a purpose with regard to the human race. This god is the soul of the world; each of us is gifted with a spark of the divine fire. Each life is good when it is in accord with nature, for nature caused it to be. But each human will must submit to this nature. Virtue consists in directing one's will to the ends desired by nature. Virtue is a word which has changed its meaning over time. When used by the Ancient Greeks it meant the practice of human excellence.

### Determinism and freedom

We can now see that the important core of stoic teaching involves determinism and human freedom. Virtue is the only thing that counts in the life of each individual person. Health, wealth and the pursuit of happiness do not count. Virtue is in the will. One can be poor, ill, persecuted, but outsiders can only affect the externals. From this it follows that all have full freedom, as long as they free themselves from false desires and become indifferent to them. No outside force can rob individuals of their virtue.

So the stoic learns to be indifferent to all external influences: good and evil depend on the self alone. If one can learn to be indifferent to events, they will have no power over one. Only the will is good or bad. Stoicism placed responsibility for becoming a good or bad person entirely on the individual. Society could never be blamed for such an outcome.

### Stoic indifference

But stoicism was a cold philosophy, an ethic of indifference. All passions were condemned. It was one's duty to engage in public life for it provided the opportunity to follow virtue, promote justice, practise courage and determination. But one did this in order to be virtuous;

the idea of helping other members of the human race, of seeking happiness or of promoting a creative, active and supportive community did not come into the picture.

Nevertheless, many of the people who practised stoicism were kindly, humane individuals, who gave themselves to public service. The Roman writer Seneca (3 BCE–65 CE) was a stoic, as was the Roman emperor Marcus Aurelius (121–180 CE).

## Appraisal

Can stoicism be criticized because of its teaching about free will and determinism? On the one hand Zeno taught cosmic determinism, on the other he thought that virtue resides in the exercise of the will. The problem of reconciling free will and determinism does not just appear in stoicism, however. It has long been a problem in philosophy, in ethics and in Christian theology. It has never been suitably resolved.

Stoics taught that everything that happens – the falling of a leaf, the crash of two trains, the decision to go to war in Iraq – is inevitably decided beforehand. We cannot alter our circumstances. Therefore we cannot alter our character or get a grip on ourselves and make a change for the better. Does this resonate with you? If not, how would you mount a *reasoned* objection?

This is still a problem in modern popular psychology and often arises in criminal law cases. If we are all totally determined and Joe Bloggs murders his neighbour, then a true stoic must say that this was inevitable because of Joe's past history, the circumstances he grew up in, his heredity, the situation he now found himself in and that he cannot be held responsible for his actions. In short, despite all appearances, Joe Bloggs was not a free man; none of us is a free person. However, if we stress the exercise of the will we may come to a different conclusion. What is more, there may be different meanings of freedom used in the paragraph above. If 'freedom' and 'free' mean something different in different sentences and contexts above, then that argument is not valid.

When I say I am 'free' what do I mean? I am free now at this moment to go and buy a packet of sweets. I am free to do so because I can afford them and because I have the free time to do so. So I am free. On the other hand I am not free to fly. I do not have wings. So I am not free. I am not free to murder my neighbour: the laws and moral feeling prevent me. So I am not free. Am I free or not? Broad general statements unlinked to any context whatsoever can be misleading. Can you think of other meanings of 'free', and where they might apply?

The stoic teaching about indifference seems to lack common sense. Is it right to develop a sense of indifference without cultivating other feelings and virtues? Is it right to be indifferent when someone we love and value is going through a difficult time? Does an incorrect action, for instance stealing, become 'moral' if it is done 'indifferently', if we have no affective involvement in it, if we receive no benefit from it?

Stoic philosophy seems to appeal only in extreme circumstances. Is it therefore a philosophy that can be raised to the level of a universal ethic? Indifference may help us if we are in unusually difficult circumstances, held hostage for example. But is it normal or right to expect a man or woman in such a situation to be indifferent to what comes next? Is it a moral advance if they do not worry about the wife or husband, children, friends or relatives at home? Should the relatives at home develop a state of indifference about the one held captive?

Nevertheless, there are useful pointers for particular contexts here. If those responsible for crisis-management are too emotionally involved in what is happening they will not perform efficiently. They must impose a discipline of self-control, of distance, of level-headedness in difficult situations. This applies to many situations in everyday living as experienced by police, fire brigade members, ambulance staff, nursing and other medical workers.

On the other hand, if all is well in life, it seems silly to be indifferent to it when such moments might be enjoyed.

Stoicism is a philosophy of consolation. The Christian St Paul, when he was in prison, cried out, 'I have learned, in whatsoever state I am, therewith to be content.' He spoke there as would a courageous stoic.

# 4 Thomas Aquinas: the Unified Interpretation of Reality

With Thomas Aquinas we take a look at one of the great Christian philosophers. Christianity had not lacked learned men before him (one thinks of men such as St Ambrose, St Jerome, St Augustine and pope Gregory the Great – all four are known as Doctors of the Western Church), nor has Christianity lacked them since. But the teachings and writings of St Thomas Aquinas were to become the cornerstone of Christian education in the West. They were the staple diet of a young man's training for the priesthood, particularly in the Roman Catholic tradition. Thomas Aquinas's philosophy is known as 'Thomism' (from Thomas). His published works in modern format take up several yards of shelf space, originally written (it is thought) in the brief space of twenty years. Aquinas is frequently given the honorific title of *Doctor angelicus.* (The word 'doctor' here has nothing to do with medicine and comes from the old Latin word for teacher; the common usage

Thomas Aquinas

nevertheless is to translate it as 'Angelic Doctor'.) In the twentieth century there has been a revival of interest in his works and his methods are applied to the culture of the contemporary world. This movement is known as neothomism.

## Life

Thomas's father was Count of Aquino. Thomas was born in a castle near Naples in 1225 and was sent at the age of 5 to be educated at the famous Benedictine Abbey of Monte Cassino. He remained there until 1239. He entered the University of Naples at the age of 14. When he was 20 he entered the Dominican order. This seriously upset his family, and Thomas was kidnapped by his brothers and held prisoner in the family castle for about a year. The story goes that his family introduced a young and beautiful girl into his room in the hope that he might develop a taste for the delights of the flesh and turn away from his priestly calling; but the unusual young man drove her angrily from the room, quoting psalms.

Thomas was determined to remain true to his vocation, and eventually he managed to escape and resume his studies, this time at the University of Paris. Here he came under the influence of St Albert the Great, a most erudite teacher who was full of intellectual curiosity. Albert was particularly interested in the works of Aristotle. This was to have a profound effect on the development of the thought of Thomas Aquinas. Some say that Thomas may not have had the same sense of open curiosity as his teacher, but he certainly possessed unique powers of systematization. Thomas was to succeed in expressing Christian thought in terms of Aristotelian philosophy. Until the twentieth century his approach and Aristotle's thought were to be the vehicles by which Roman Catholic teaching was expressed and handed on. However, the process was not without the risk of abuse.

Thomas was to stay in Paris until 1248, before moving to Cologne, where a new Dominican house of studies (*studium generale*: an old term for university) was being established. He stayed there until 1252.

Returning to Paris, he continued his biblical studies and in 1256 completed his commentary on the *Sentences* of Peter Lombard, which was an exercise required for the Licenciate, the degree that allowed him to teach theology. He was passed Magister in the same year.

In 1259 Thomas went to Italy where he taught theology at a *studium generale* attached to the papal court. He returned to Paris in 1268, remaining there until 1272. He was in Naples setting up another *studium generale* during 1272–74. He was then summoned to Lyons by the pope to take part in a council, but died on the way at the age of 49.

Thomas Aquinas devoted his life to study, to the defence of Roman Catholic orthodoxy, to the rigorous systematization of Catholic truth and to writing. It is said that it was his custom to dictate to three different secretaries simultaneously. (Other sources suggest four.) One story holds that continuous study and lack of exercise made him very fat, so a large semi-circle had to be carved out of his work-table to accommodate his belly. Another portrait puts him as large and fat, very tall, plump with blond hair and dark complexion, slightly bald, but robust enough to have covered (on foot) the 15,000 kilometres that took him from Naples to Paris, thence to Cologne and back to Paris again, to Rome and back, and from there once more to Naples.

He was a man of piety and spirituality, with great devotion to the eucharist and the humanity of Christ. Those who pleaded the cause of his canonization presented him as of smiling countenance, gentle and affable, with rare humility and patience, never upsetting anyone with harsh words. He was invited by pope Urban IV to compose the daily office for the new feast of Corpus Christi, which celebrates the institution and gift of the eucharist. (Its observance was commanded in 1264.)

Thomas's two great works are the *Summa contra Gentiles* (1258–1260), which sets out to establish the truth of the Christian religion by argument addressed to a thinker who is not a Christian (possibly a Muslim Arab) and the *Summa Theologiae* (more frequently called *Summa Theologica*: 1265–74). He thought and wrote at a time when Christianity was challenged by a vigorous Islam, from which it had also much to learn, and Thomas's own achievements are evidence of this.

Thomas Aquinas is buried in Toulouse, in the Eglise des Jacobins. He was canonized (declared a saint) by pope John XXII in 1323. His feast-day used to be 7 March but is now 28 January.

---

**Timeline**

1180–1170  Averroes' commentaries on Aristotle

1215  Magna Carta

1217  Start of the Fifth Crusade

1225  Birth of Thomas Aquinas

1226  Louis IX (St Louis) becomes King of France

1230  Education of Thomas at Monte Cassino

1239  Thomas at the University of Naples

1245  Thomas enters the Dominican order and is 'kidnapped' by his family

1246  Thomas a pupil of Albert the Great in Paris

1248  In Cologne with Albert the Great

1256  Thomas gains degrees

1257  Founding of the Sorbonne

1258–60  Thomas writing the *Summa contra Gentiles*

1259  Thomas teaches at a college attached to the papal court

1265–74  Thomas writing the *Summa Theologica*

1271  Marco Polo begins his travels in China

1272  Thomas sets up a college in Naples

1274  Dies *en route* to a council in Lyons

---

## Thought

### A Christian philosopher

It might be helpful to see if we can get some basic notion of what is meant when we talk about both philosophy and theology.

Theology is an attempt to organize the doctrines of religion in a systematic fashion. Religion is the expression of how we see the ultimate nature of reality: some of its elements are rational, some not. (Note: when we say they are not rational, we just mean they are non-rational. This is not the same as saying they are irrational.) The non-rational elements contain intuitions, emotions and the surrender of self to God in worship. Such elements depend on the content of the 'revelation' of religion: information or knowledge considered to have come from a divine source. How people reflect on these elements, work out values, give balanced importance to the teaching of holy books and holy teachers, consider questions of right and wrong, plan and develop liturgy and worship in the light of what they have thought about are all rational elements of religion.

Theology assumes that religion is a valid and authentic human activity; its basic premises are those of faith (non-rational). Theology organizes the ideas involved in religion into a rational, logical and coherent system. It exists to enquire into the implications of faith and to sift out what is not consistent with its truth and values.

Philosophy assumes nothing except that all experience can be examined in a rational manner. It tries to give a coherent, consistent, comprehensive account of our human experience and of the world in which we live. This is done with the aid of reason, not revelation. There is a very clear tension between the two ways of thinking. While religion finds its most important expression in surrender to an object of worship (God), philosophers will not find it possible to surrender themselves to an unverifiable hypothesis.

Nevertheless, some coming closer is possible. The theologian argues that spirit is the true source of all existence and that spirit maintains a true fellowship with all who depend on it. The theologian must therefore (in true philosophical mode) distinguish carefully between all elements that have real spiritual importance and those elements which have merely traditional and emotional value. The philosopher accepts the methods of science and notes that science does not concern itself with values. A philosophy of religion is only possible when we accept the fact that intuition and a sense of values are part of the reality we wish to investigate.

## The development of systematic Christian thought

Plato was a thinker of great originality and profundity: he could absorb the ideas of those who went before him and from them extract deeper meanings and implications. He did not organize his philosophy into a system, but neither did he leave a selection of discordant and unconnected ideas. Nevertheless, Plato aimed at reaching a complete system in which all questions could be addressed.

The early Christian Fathers saw much in Plato that they could use, and were anxious to use the intellectual language of Platonism to express the newly emerging Christian engagement with the world. They appreciated his distinction between the world of sense and the world of the eternal forms; how he identified these forms with the thoughts of God. They liked his moral earnestness and his view that the great aim of the human soul is the search for the good. They rejected such ideas as the notion of reminiscence in his theory of knowledge. (This implied that the soul existed before in another life, whereas Christianity holds that each individual is unique and valuable in the sight of God.) They also abandoned his theory of reminiscence as being the source of values, and his way of looking at immortality, which ran counter to the Christian doctrine of the resurrection.

The early Fathers were less positive about Aristotle as his materialistic bias did not appeal to them. Virtue, which for Aristotle, consisted of moderation, did not resonate with the Christian idea of love (*Caritas*). Aristotle's God (the prime mover) was too far removed from a loving God's mortal creatures. Aristotle's thought was neglected by early Christians and was later lost. Only a few works were known and these were often in imperfect copies. However, most of the important works of Aristotle had been preserved in the great libraries of the Arab world, and it was not until the times were right for fruitful contact between the Christian West and the Arab East that Aristotle's works would be known in greater detail and in better versions. When the great Arab philosophers Avicenna (980–1037) and Averroes (1126–1280) blended Aristotle's thought with that of Plato, interest was awakened in the Christian West. The prime mover of this renewed interest was Albert the Great, followed by his pupil Thomas Aquinas.

### Thomas's contribution to theology

Thomas Aquinas was convinced that faith and reason were quite distinct. If a truth was grasped by faith then it was a gift of divine revelation. A truth reached by reason, might also be the gift of revelation, but he held that human reason does have the power to reach certain truths unaided by revelation's light. The soul was illuminated by God and thus able to grasp eternal truths intellectually. It was possible to start with the external world and to argue by reason to the existence of God. The creative power of God, the eternity of God and the providence of God could all be proved in this way without the help of revelation. God might be known through his sensible effects.

Thomas wholeheartedly adopted the Aristotelian principle that all knowledge starts from sense-perception: '*Nihil in intellectu quod non prius fuerit in sensu*' (The intellect contains nothing that was not first in the senses). The five ways of Thomas Aquinas (also called the theistic arguments) are logical proofs of the existence of God. Thomas considered such proofs to be necessary, since any innate knowledge we have of God is too vague and confused to constitute a clear and distinct reasoning. His arguments are all *a posteriori* arguments: from effects back to cause.

---

### *Summa contra Gentiles* (1260)

- Wise men are those who deal with the first beginnings and the last end of the universe. Truth is the final end, and if one wants to understand first and last things one must first of all consider the divine nature.

- No truths of faith are contrary to principles known by reason.
- We understand temporally, but God understands eternally. God does not understand by knowing an object directly, but by knowing its intelligible counterpart in his own understanding: understanding all things together and at once. God knows individuals as well as universals.
- The only cause of God's will is the divine wisdom, so God's will is free having no cause outside itself. God of necessity loves himself, but does not love other things of necessity.
- God has no potentiality: God is active power. God is essentially infinite; God's knowledge and understanding are infinite.
- Since human beings are rational creatures, their final happiness lies in the contemplation of God: an end which cannot be achieved in this life.

*Proofs of the existence of God*

St Anselm (1033–1109) had proposed an argument for the existence of God. It came in the form of a prayer in which he addressed to God his conviction that God, 'a being than which no greater can be conceived', must exist. If God were simply an idea and thought of as non-existent, it would be a contradiction because a God that existed would be greater than the idea of one. But if God is one 'than which no greater can be conceived' then God must inevitably exist. This is known as the ontological argument.

Thomas Aquinas rejected this argument on the grounds that Anselm's definition of God ('than which no greater can be conceived') is not what everybody means by God. This reply is not now highly considered: Anselm meant the supremely perfect being. It seems, in addition, to ignore a similar defect: in his own definition of God as one whose 'essence is to exist'. Secondly, Thomas held that Anselm's argument involved making a transition 'from the real to the ideal order', and that this involved a logical fallacy. Thirdly, he argued that the intellect has no *a priori* knowledge of God. It cannot argue forward out of its own resources to the existence of God. So Aquinas proceeded to elaborate a series of *a posteriori* arguments: backwards from effects to cause.

> - An *a priori* argument, concept, statement or judgement is one which is not based on experience, on the five senses. The notion of *valid* might be arrived at by *a priori* reasoning
> - An *a posteriori* argument, concept, statement or judgement is based on experience, on the five senses.
> - An efficient cause is the outside agency or process working on matter (or on a situation) that causes change to take place.
> - A final cause is the final outcome an agent has in mind when initiating change.

Aristotle had already anticipated some of these arguments. Nevertheless they received their classical shape and statement with Thomas Aquinas.

> ### The five ways of Thomas Aquinas
>
> 1. *The unmoved mover* Everything is in movement, so something must have started that movement. To find this starting-point we cannot keep taking one step back for ever, a series of moved movers must have had a beginning in a mover who was not moved. This unmoved mover we call God.
> 2. *The first cause* Everything has a cause. Cause not merely precedes but actively produces its effect. But there must have been a starting-point (terminus) that actively willed and produced all that there is. This first cause we call God.
> 3. *The argument from contingency* Many things exist though nothing in their nature requires them to exist; they come into being and pass away; they are dispensable. In this case there must have been a time when nothing existed unless there was some necessary being to account for them. This being who must necessarily exist to account for all contingent beings, we call God.

4. *The argument from degrees of being* Things either exist or they do not. When we say metaphorically that some things are more real than others we mean they are richer in content and significance. This ascending scale of being, truth and goodness must have a limit, a being who has these qualities to a supreme degree. This being we call God.

5. *The argument from design* The world as we observe it shows signs of design and purpose. This overarching design and purpose indicates a designer whom we call God.

In modern times these arguments have been severely criticized by Christian theologians and philosophers of religion. In the first four arguments (from movement, from efficient causality, from contingency and degrees of being), God is treated as one being among others that exist. Nevertheless, each of the descriptions is fundamentally qualified. God is *unmoved* mover, *first* cause, *necessary* being: the superlative which is the *source* of qualities in all things. Thus God is removed from each series of items or events from which deity is deduced, and the arguments show the divine being to be of a different order from the series of entities from which the *a posteriori* arguments arise. (This was one of the criticisms Thomas made of Anselm.)

The fifth (teleological) argument is of a different type: all things are directed to a goal by *aliquis intelligens* (an intelligent being). Even if this is imprecise in Thomas's writing it is implied in his reasoning. The final outcome is that God is the efficient cause of the universe and its intelligent ruler. Even if these arguments cannot logically establish the existence of God, they all stress a monarchical conception of God as creator, ruler, first cause and providence. They stress what we mean by 'God'.

## *Summa Theologica* (1274)

• Human persons require more than philosophy in their search for truth. Some truths are beyond human understanding and only available to us because God has revealed them. Theology depends on revealed knowledge and supplements natural knowledge. The existence of God may be proved in five ways: from the facts of motion, efficient causes, possibility and necessity, gradations of perfection in the world, the order and harmony of the world.

- God alone can account for the fact of motion, efficient cause, necessity, perfection and order.
- We describe God as being simple (noncorporeal and without genus), actual, perfect, good, infinite, unchanging, one, present in the world. It is by God's grace alone that human persons, as created beings, can know God. We can only grasp God; we cannot understand God (through apprehension, not through comprehension).

### The doctrine of analogy: how can we talk about God?

How can we say anything about God? If we say God is our father this suggests that God has a head, two hands and two arms, that God is male. But God is held to be spirit, not body, God has no sex, is personal but neither male nor female. So people tend to say, 'You say God is our father, but that's not what you mean, so why do you say it?' This is because they are using language *univocally* as if each word only had one fixed meaning. So then people begin to think, 'Oh, he says one thing but wants you to believe something different!' This is using language *equivocally*, using double meanings. To get over such problems Thomas Aquinas elaborated his theory of analogy.

We may say that a holiday destination is a lively resort; we may say that a person is a lively person. When we say the resort is lively, we do not mean that it is vivacious, likes telling jokes, laughs a lot, likes to go dancing and such like. We mean that in this resort all the facilities exist for lively people to enjoy themselves and that they do enjoy themselves when they go there. The description of the resort is analogical. When we say that a town is a lively resort or that a certain group is a lively group the meanings come from a 'prime analogate': a lively person. But we cannot use prime analogates with regard to God, for nothing is antecedent to God to which God may be compared.

All valid statements about God are analogical. When we say that God is our father, God is neither wholly like a human father nor wholly unlike a human father.

We use the analogy of proportionality which states that properties of created beings are related to their existence in the manner appropriate to the existence of a created being. On the other hand, properties of uncreated being are related to its existence in the manner appropriate to uncreated being.

We may use the analogy of attribution, which describes a relation obtaining between God and his creatures by using terms drawn from the relationships that hold between creatures. When we say, 'God is Father', we are not speaking anthropomorphically (as if God were human). We are not speaking symbolically. This manner of speaking rather illustrates the relationship of dependence between creature and creator by using the analogy of child and father.

### Thomas Aquinas's philosophy

Generally, the philosophy of Thomas Aquinas agrees with the philosophy of Aristotle. He is original in the way he adapts Aristotle to Christian apologetics. He knows Aristotle well and understands him. Many have considered him a systematizer rather than an original thinker. Both his *Summas* are imposing systematic and intellectual edifices. He is very sharp and clear in his writing; doctrines, including those he wishes to refute, are stated clearly and fairly. He distinguishes clearly arguments derived from faith and arguments derived from reason.

### The philosophical method of the schoolmen

The schoolmen were the teachers of philosophy and theology in the Middle Ages. From the writings of Thomas Aquinas and others, but particularly from those of Thomas, a whole manner of dealing with intellectual questions was elaborated. It was quite formal. A student would be asked to state a thesis (an argument, a truth). Then the student would supply a proof of the thesis, using scripture and tradition, faith and *magisterium* (the authoritative teaching of the Roman Catholic Church). Then the student would reject the opposite position, also on the basis of scripture, the Church Fathers and other authoritative sources. Finally, the student would give a speculative elaboration.

Here is an example of this sort of procedure. *Thesis*: 'Outside of the Church there is no salvation.' The thesis is stated. This will now be proved by quotations from scripture (e.g., 'No one comes to the Father except by me' John 14.6). This would be further backed up by quotations from the Fathers (St Thomas himself became a favourite source of supporting quotations) and from writings of the popes. The opposite would next be stated: 'Some say you can be saved no matter what religion you accept.' This would be rejected and reasons given, again with quotes from scripture, the Fathers and popes. Finally, the thesis would be given a speculative elaboration: the student would speculate on what happens to schismatics, apostates and the unbaptized; on the existence of heaven, hell, limbo, purgatory, and so forth. The theory was that if one could find an intellectual answer the problem was solved; all was well.

### Thomism

Today the philosophy of Aquinas occupies a favoured position in the Roman Catholic Church. In 1879 pope Leo XIII asserted the permanent value of Thomas's synthesis and urged all Catholics to draw their inspiration from him, while at the same time developing Thomism to meet contemporary needs. There has been a long process of 'extracting' a philosophical system from the works of one who never could have imagined such a system in isolation from theology. Thomas Aquinas had both a profound belief in the Christian religion and also a real trust in the power of the human mind and in the value of philosophical reflection. Today Thomism is very much concerned with reflecting on the concrete act of apprehending what exists objectively and also on the metaphysical conditions and implications of that act.

Modern Thomists are probably more interested in continental philosophy of the speculative kind rather than the analytical philosophy more favoured in English-speaking universities.

## Appraisal

Aquinas created a two-tier intellectual system. He effected a sharp separation between theology and philosophy. Philosophy deals with many of the questions dealt with by theology, but does so in its own manner and using its own tools: free rational enquiry and argument. Aquinas was sure that, ultimately, faith and reason could not clash. Do you agree? How do you see them eliding or colliding?

Aquinas was an Aristotelian; he set out from sense-perception. The separation of faith and reason and the acceptance of the senses as the source of human knowledge were decisive for the development of philosophy as a discipline. All previous Christian philosophers had explained the effect by the cause. Thomas started with the effect. He did not explain God starting with God's transcendence. He began with what could be known about the creatures.

Earlier Christian philosophers had baulked at Aristotle because they could not reconcile the transitory nature of the world with the eternity of God. Terms such as form and matter, act and potentiality all represented a world of becoming. For centuries such terms stood in contrast to the permanence and unchanging attributes of God. We have had to wait until the twentieth century to see such a vocabulary of process applied to God. How and why might that be interesting?

Nowadays it might be said by modern Thomists that philosophy gives us an empty form, Christian faith fills it with content. Does philosophy always give an empty form; does it always need a value-system to fill it with content?

Thomas Aquinas's principle of analogy is often severely criticized; it cannot be established by argument but it presupposes that human language does not lose its validity when applied to God. Try to note other approaches to the problem of 'God-talk'.

# 5 René Descartes: Systematic Doubt as a Philosophical Method

In earlier times the most important entity was either the state (the Greek city-state) or the Church. Nowadays it tends to be the individual, and not just any individual but ME! Have you ever wondered how the self came to be at the centre of our concerns in the modern age? Blame Descartes, say the philosophers. But is this fair?

## Life

René Descartes was born in the village of La Haye in 1596. This village is about 35 miles south of the city of Tours in central France. (You won't find it on the map any longer because it has been renamed in honour of the philosopher and mathematician.) The house in which Descartes was born is now a tiny museum at 29 rue Descartes, in the village of Descartes.

René Descartes

At the age of 8, Descartes was sent to the nearby Jesuit college of La Flèche (now a military academy). He remained there for eight years, studying logic, philosophy and mathematics. He was a gifted and eager pupil. He was, however, quite a delicate boy and was often allowed to stay late in bed in order to rest. It is said that on such an occasion, while watching a spider construct a web, he worked out the principles of coordinate geometry. He was, in later life, grateful to the Jesuits for the education he had received, and believed it to have been of extremely high quality.

Descartes resolved to study in 'the great book of the world', and decided to take up a military career, mostly outside France. A military career seems a very odd choice for one whose health was so delicate. However, he saw military service in Germany, Bavaria, Hungary and Bohemia. It is said he accepted no pay for his military service, and combined army life with the study of mathematics, philosophy and music. Descartes reputedly had several dreams which eventually persuaded him that his mission in life was to seek the truth by means of reason. In thanksgiving for this revelation he resolved to go on a pilgrimage to the house of Our Lady of Loreto in Italy; however, he didn't make the visit until much later. He lived in Paris for a while, but is said to have found it distracting.

Descartes wrote a number of books. These were quickly translated into French at a time when learned people still corresponded in Latin. Among his works were *Treatise on the World, Discourse on Method, Meditations on First Philosophy* and *Passions of the Soul*. He delayed the publication of his *Treatise on the World* because Galileo had been condemned by the Inquisition for false teaching. Descartes lived mostly in Holland, and this may have been because censorship there was less strict than elsewhere.

In 1649 Descartes accepted an invitation to visit the court of Queen Christina of Sweden, who was anxious to learn modern philosophy. However, the harsh Swedish winter was bad for his health. The Queen also expected him to conduct his lessons at five o'clock in the morning! This was all too much for poor Descartes: he was used to lying in bed thinking until quite late in the day. He became ill with a fever and died on 11 February 1650, after only five months in Sweden. Descartes never married. He was a quiet, retiring gentleman, said to be kind and generous to his servants. He was a devout Roman Catholic, yet intent on occupying himself with problems which could be solved by reason alone. He consciously set out to construct a new philosophical system.

---

**Intuition** is the immediate grasping of truth without the aid of reasoning.

**Deduction** is drawing conclusions by a process of reasoning from established facts; a series of propositions following definite rules, drawn from the axioms and rules of inference.

**Epistemology** is that part of philosophy which studies the history, methods and principles of knowledge.

**Ontology** is the study of being as being, being in itself.

**Cartesian method** is the philosophical method of Descartes. (Des*cartes* = *Cartes*ian)

---

**Timeline**

1591  Introduction of the use of letters to represent quantities in
         algebra
1592  Galileo invents the thermometer
1596  Birth of Descartes
1603  Death of Elizabeth I
1604–12  Descartes at college at La Flèche
c. 1614–26  Descartes as a soldier/philosopher
1614  Napier's logarithms
1618  Start of Thirty Years' War
1619  (10th November) the day in the stove
1620  Francis Bacon's *New Organon*
c. 1626–28  Descartes in Paris

1628–49  Descartes in Holland

1637  Descartes' *Discourse on Method*

1638  Galileo's law on the movement of the pendulum

1641  Descartes' *Meditations on First Philosophy*

1643  Louis XIV King of France

1649  Descartes' *Treatise on the Passions*

1649–50  Descartes in Sweden

1650  Death of Descartes

## Thought

### *The slow arrival of modernity*

Between the Renaissance and the nineteenth century, control of culture slowly became the business of the state rather than the Church. Government steadily came to have more influence in many areas of life. Many national states replaced their kings (said to have received their authority from God) with other forms of government. The trading classes increasingly got their hands on the levers of power. The new culture was, in the main, 'liberal'. The new institutions never sought to control philosophers to the extent that the medieval Church did.

This modern era had a new outlook. There were two gradual but obvious changes. The first was the decline in the authority of the Church, in particular (but not only) that of the Roman Catholic Church. The second was the growing authority of science.

The new science appealed to reason. It was piecemeal, making its discoveries in small steps; it no longer wished to lay down a complete system. The pronouncements of the medieval Church were made as if they were announcing absolute truth. New scientific truths were announced tentatively, on the basis of probability, and were open to correction and change. The temper of the new scientific mind was questing rather than authoritarian. The society in which such values are foremost tends to be a dynamic society, with fewer fixed points of reference, and a smaller number of certainties. The scientific outlook tends to be ethically neutral.

Modern philosophy still has a subjective leaning. This is quite obvious in Descartes who built up all knowledge on the basis of the certainty of his own existence.

### The founder of modern philosophy

Descartes is quite rightly considered to be the founder of modern philosophy. He was the first philosopher of high, inventive ability to be influenced by the new physics and astronomy. He wrote not as a teacher but as an explorer. His style was lively rather than stuffy.

Descartes was determined to reinvent philosophy from the beginning, relying on reason alone, without trusting the authority of any philosopher who had gone before. He wanted to avoid all conjecture and rely only on what was clear and evident. He was convinced that he must work with clear, distinct, abstract ideas. He spoke of intuition and deduction as the most certain routes to knowledge. It is important to note that Descartes was looking for the order of *knowing*, not the order of *being*. For him the important enquiry concerned epistemology rather than ontology. Thus we may claim that the modern era in philosophy began with Descartes.

### The day in the stove

Modern philosophy began on 10 November 1619, the day that Descartes spent in a stove and came out with 'the idea of a universal method for discovering truth'.

How could he have spent a day in a stove? What did he mean? Various suggestions have been put forward. It may have been a small room which was heated with a stove, possibly the only heated room in the house. On the other hand, the fireplace may have been in an alcove with the chimneybreast jutting well out into the room, so that one sat in the alcove, under the mantelpiece, beside the fire. Whatever it was, it was there that modern philosophy was born.

It was in that stove in Germany that Descartes decided to make a clean sweep, to do away with all scholastic philosophy and to start afresh. From it came the first great philosophical and scientific work to be published in a modern language (French rather than Latin). Descartes wanted it to be accessible to 'those who use only their natural reason in its pure state'. The book was called *Discourse on Method*, and in it Descartes laid out the four rules of his method. It is to them that we now turn.

---

### The Cartesian rules

The fact that one has lots of rules, observed Descartes, is often an excuse for not getting things right. (He felt that a state was often better ruled when it had fewer rather than many laws.) Therefore he resolved to have only four rules. When modern politicians talk of the advantages of 'deregulation' they unconsciously echo Descartes.

1. He accepted nothing as true unless he knew it evidently to be so. He would accept nothing unless it presented itself so clearly and distinctly to his judgement that he had no reason to doubt it. This is the rule of clear and distinct ideas.
2. He divided each of the problems he examined into as many elementary subdivisions as he could, and as were necessary to resolve the problem. This is the rule of analysis.
3. He conducted his thoughts in an ordered manner. He would start with the simplest and easiest ideas to understand. He would progress by degrees towards the most complicated. This is the rule of progression from the simple to the complex.
4. He carried out such complete and frequent reviews that he was certain to have left nothing out. This is the rule of synthesis.

It is important to note that thinking a problem through involves two major movements of the mind: *analysis* and *synthesis*.

- *Analysis*: breaking down the problem into clearly understood elements.
- *Synthesis*: placing all the elements together so that one gets an overall picture.

## The method of systematic doubt

In order to have a totally secure basis on which he could build his new philosophy Descartes decided that he would doubt everything that could possibly be doubted. He noted that it was possible to be deceived with regard to what our senses tell us. Sometimes my table looks very dark brown, sometimes very light brown; it often depends on which way the light is shining on it and, indeed, on how strong the light is. So which is the right way to describe the colour of my table? It is possible to be deceived with regard to the nature of one's body. People who have had an arm or a leg amputated often feel a pain or an itch, apparently in the missing limb. Their bodies have deceived them. It is possible to be deceived with regard to the subject-matter of mathematics. We've all got our sums wrong! Am I even deceived about my own existence? Is there anything at all that cannot be doubted?

## 'I think, therefore I am'

Yes, there is something that cannot be doubted, said Descartes. I am sitting here doubting everything. If I am doubting, I must exist! 'I think, therefore I am.' ('*Je pense, donc je suis.*') One of the most famous phrases in the French language, it is generally known the world over in its Latin form: '*Cogito, ergo sum.*' The argument is often referred to as 'the *Cogito*'.

But there is a further problem: can being exist quite apart from the knowledge we have of it? Descartes put forward thinking as the fundamental certainty about existence. It was the only immediate datum. This is the way he had started all over again from the very beginning. But from now on all existence would appear to depend on the existence of thinking, which was easier to know than any other form of existence. Descartes was happy to say that thought was the only *immediate* reality. Some of his rationalist successors would say it was the *only* reality!

Descartes made mind more certain than matter, and my mind (for me) more certain than any other mind. Why was he so sure that his *Cogito* was correct? Because it was clear and distinct. What did Descartes mean by 'thinking'? 'Everything that is done in such a way that we perceive it immediately by ourselves; that is why not just understanding, willing, imagining, but also feeling is the same thing as thinking.'

---

### *Discourse on Method* (1637)

- Correct philosophical method is only to accept ideas that are clear and distinct and therefore cannot be doubted; to divide complex questions into simple basic questions; to proceed from the simple to the complex; to review all steps in reasoning.
- When one puts this method into practice one must doubt all propositions except: 'I think, therefore I am.'
- I am a thinking substance who has an idea of God. I could not have derived the idea of a perfect being from my own experience, so God must exist as the source of my idea. Imperfect contingent beings could not exist without a perfect being. God must necessarily exist, for if he did not he would not be a perfect being.
- The God who exists provides the ground for our knowledge about the external world, but we must only accept those ideas that are clear and distinct and beyond doubt, for the reliability of the senses and reason derives from God.

---

### *Body and mind*

Descartes decided that he was essentially a thinking being. From there he worked out that the soul or mind (that part of him which did the thinking) was totally separate and distinct from his body, and also easier to know than his body.

He saw the mind and the body as running parallel, but not connected. One way to grasp his idea is to think of two alarm clocks standing side by side. The first alarm clock has no bell, but it has hands; the second alarm clock has no hands but has a bell. When the set time shows on the first alarm clock, the bell on the second clock rings. But they are not connected. Mind and body are not connected; they only appear to be.

Think of a piece of wax, said Descartes, its qualities are apparent to the touch. These qualities change under different conditions: heat the wax and it gets soft; cool it and it gets hard. These qualities are not the wax itself, said Descartes. This is understood by the mind, not perceived by the senses. Knowledge of objects must therefore come about through the mind, not the senses.

## Proof of the existence of God

Descartes cast doubt on everything to do with the external world. He affirmed his own existence because he was a thinking being. His own existence could be grasped immediately in the act of thinking. What about that reality which can be observed by means of the senses? Its existence also needs to be demonstrated. Descartes did this by calling on God. Only the existence of a perfect being, who was incapable of deception, assured him that the existence of external bodies was not an illusion.

On what philosophical grounds did Descartes believe in God? If one is alert to the fact that one is doubting, he said, one is aware of imperfection. We know about this imperfection as soon as we realize we make mistakes. But being aware of imperfection implies the idea of perfection. The idea of perfection could not have its origin in an imperfect being. Only an infinite and perfect being could cause the idea of perfection.

This is a version of an old idea, originally put forward in the Middle Ages by Anselm, that existence is an essential part of perfection. If something is perfect and does not exist, then it is less than perfect, and to that extent is a contradiction in terms. This is known as the onto-logical argument for the existence of God.

An imperfect being (such as a human person) is of necessity dependent upon the power of a perfect being (such as God). Imperfect beings depend both for their original existence and their continuing existence, hour by hour, upon a perfect being.

## *What is rationalism?*

Descartes was a rationalist philosopher. Rationalists are contrasted with empiricists. (We will be looking at empiricism when we discuss David Hume in Chapter 8.) What is meant by rationalism?

There are some statements that have to be true: they could not pos-sibly be false. Likewise, there are some statements that have to be false. Take for example: 'One can't be in two places at the same time.' This is a necessary truth. What makes it a necessary truth? It is know-able *a priori*. That means that it has to hold true for all cases and just thinking about what it means will display its truth.

Other statements just happen to be true. They are contingent. How many people are in the room with you as you read? The number could vary. There is no one number that *has* to be true. Look up from the book and count! This is the only way you can check the number of people in the room with you. This means that the number of people in the room with you now is knowable *a posteriori*: check it out and you have your answer. With an *a priori* statement you don't have to look up. You know already that it *has* to be true or false. Looking up and checking is an example of *empirical verification*. *A priori* statements don't need empirical verification.

But do *a priori* statements give us information, or are they just another way of defining what has already been said? Such statements are said to be analytic: 'A dog is a dog.' 'A square has four sides.' 'Quadrupeds have four legs.' What each of these statements does is restate what has already been said. It is part of the definition of a square that it has four sides. It is part of the definition of a quadruped that it has four legs. Analytic statements just repeat in different words what you already know. They do not give us new information.

A synthetic statement gives you new information: 'There are 50 states in the United States of America.' 'Napoleon was defeated in 1815.' 'The Taj Mahal is in India.' None of those statements restates in other words what has already been said. None of them *has* to be true. They all give information. (Check and you'll see!) They are synthetic statements.

Are all synthetic statements contingent, knowable *a posteriori*? And are all analytic statements necessary, known *a priori*? Or are there such things as synthetic *a priori* statements: statements which give us fresh information but which are necessarily true?

Empiricists claim that there are no such things as synthetic *a priori* statements. Rationalists claim that there are such things as synthetic *a priori* statements. Rationalists say that we get certain concepts from experience, but after we have got them in this way we see by 'rational insight' that they have to be the way they are. Descartes was a philosopher of rationalist outlook; the first great thinker of the modern rationalist tradition.

These notions will be particularly important when we look at David Hume and Immanuel Kant.

Appraisal

We can see that even though he resolved to make a total break with the past, Descartes carried with him a number of notions from the scholastic philosophy of the Middle Ages. We see this in the way he brought God in to justify an inclination to believe in the existence of physical bodies. Nevertheless, the general thrust of his thought was innovative, radical and bold.

His rules on analysis, clarity, progress and synthesis are still useful. Anybody who is extremely methodical and rational is still thought of as possessing a Cartesian outlook. But it is important to use the rules as an aid, not as a straitjacket.

It is not possible to doubt everything. Descartes had the answer to the thoroughgoing sceptic. If one doubts everything, one's questions become meaningless. There must be a point where doubt has to stop: in facts that cannot be doubted and in rules of logic that cannot be questioned. Try to note other thinkers' approaches to these problems. Have they succeeded in finding facts that cannot be doubted and logical procedures that cannot be questioned?

Descartes' radical separation of body and mind theoretically had the advantage of making the soul independent of the body, which Christian thought of the period would have welcomed. But the separation does not agree with experience, particularly modern psychological experience.

The great mathematician, philosopher and theologian A.N. Whitehead once said, 'The ancient world takes its stand upon the drama of the universe, the modern world upon the inward drama of the soul.' Is this an improvement, and how is it significant for us as human beings in the twenty-first century?

Descartes' outlook certainly made mind more important than matter, and my mind more important than the minds of others!

# 6 Locke and Montesquieu: the Liberal State

Two radically different thinkers have been put together here, and for a very flimsy reason: they both taught a version of political philosophy promoting what we would now call the liberal state. This involved discussing ideas such as contract theory, natural law and the separation of powers. For that reason alone they sit beside each other in these pages.

Locke was a seventeenth-century middle-class Englishman. His theories were put into practice in England following the political revolution of 1688 which saw James II deposed and William of Orange crowned king. Montesquieu was an eighteenth-century Frenchman, born into what the French call the *noblesse de robe* (the family was ennobled after the Middle Ages). His ideas never really triumphed in his lifetime, and certainly not in France, though he can claim to have been one of the inspirations for the American War of Independence (1775–83) and a profound influence on the American constitution of 1787.

## Political thought after Plato and Aristotle

The great systems of political philosophy proposed by Plato and Aristotle depended on a very particular context: the Greek city-state. The Greek city-state was replaced suddenly and brutally with a totally different unit: the empire of Alexander the Great. This was quickly followed by the Roman empire, and when it in turn came to be replaced the new effectively functioning institution was the Catholic Church. The old political ideas no longer worked. The context had changed radically.

Newer forms of religion in Ancient Greece and Rome promoted the notion of personal immortality, often by mystical association with a dying god. People were admitted into these faiths by special initiation rites. After Aristotle, philosophy took on some functions that we now consider to be tasks of religion. Increasingly philosophy was instruction in how to live a good, ethical life as well as a form of personal consolation. Philosophy tinged with mystical feeling was increasingly the only outlook that compelled conviction. This tendency found in the universal Christian Church an institution that seemed ready-made for such a mindset. Without this emotional prop many felt unable to face the vastness and hostility of the world. This was the sort of outlook that citizens of Greek city-states would never have known.

Empire is a deadening form of government. The top few govern and are free; the masses obey, have no voice, are squeezed and powerless. The powerful medieval Church was experienced by ordinary people much as empire was. The break-up of this mindset and the decline in papal influence caused new fears but brought new possibilities.

The task facing all was how to live together as isolated, private human beings, but also conscious that they all shared a common human nature. Political thought now had to encompass the idea of the individual having a purely personal and private life, together with the idea of human universality: each individual endowed with a common human nature. The two notions of the 'Rights of Man' and of a universally binding rule and practice of justice have become the twin foundations of Western political civilization.

## Natural law

Gradually two notions of law developed: the law of one's locality and the universal law of reason. The law of reason was the greater. It was to provide a norm; local custom had to conform to it, as it was based on what is natural. Nature, the way things are, would give an insight into the way things ought to be. The basis for moral law, for what people should do and for what they should not do, is found in their essential nature as human beings; their nature contains indications

as to how they should live. Human beings are the only beings in
nature with the notion of 'should'. Law here does not mean the
outcome of human discussion, decision, promulgation and regulation, but rather something inbuilt. Natural law is something we discover, something that is, indeed, prior to our decisions.

## John Locke

Life

John Locke was born near Bristol, in southwestern England, in 1632.
His father was a lawyer and a Puritan who had served in parliament
with Cromwell. The young John attended Westminster School from
1646 until 1652. He then went on to study at Christ Church in
Oxford. Having graduated (both BA and MA), he was appointed a
fellow of his college and taught Greek, rhetoric and moral philosophy. The philosophy course at the University of Oxford was a form
of tired scholasticism which Locke disliked; often he could not

John Locke

see the point of the sort of questions that went with this form of reasoning.

Reading Descartes, who had also revolted against sterile scholasticism, awakened Locke's interest in a wider philosophy. (This was, however, private reading, not part of the university syllabus.) Locke developed many friendships in Oxford, amongst them Sir Robert Boyle (author of Boyle's Law), and was acquainted with many of the growing circle of modern scientific, experimental and mathematical thinkers in the university. Locke also qualified as a doctor, but never practised. He soon left Oxford to serve as secretary to a number of men influential in public life. For a while he was absent from England. When he returned he entered the service of Lord Shaftesbury, Lord Chancellor at the court of Charles I.

**Timeline**

1632  Birth of Locke
1642  Outbreak of English Civil War
1648–53  The Fronde: a revolt of French nobles against royal power
1649  Execution of Charles I; England governed by Cromwell
1651  Hobbes' *Leviathan*
1652  Locke at Oxford
1658  Death of Cromwell
1659  Locke a fellow at Christ Church
1660  Restoration of the monarchy; Charles II king
       Foundation of the Royal Society
1661  Spinoza's *Ethics*
1665  Locke working abroad as a diplomat
1666  Great Fire of London
1675–80  Locke living in France for health reasons
1681  Charles II rules without parliament
1683–88  Locke in political exile in Holland
1685  Death of Charles II; accession of the Roman Catholic James II

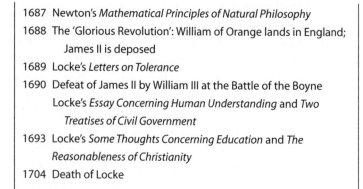

1687  Newton's *Mathematical Principles of Natural Philosophy*
1688  The 'Glorious Revolution': William of Orange lands in England;
         James II is deposed
1689  Locke's *Letters on Tolerance*
1690  Defeat of James II by William III at the Battle of the Boyne
         Locke's *Essay Concerning Human Understanding* and *Two
         Treatises of Civil Government*
1693  Locke's *Some Thoughts Concerning Education* and *The
         Reasonableness of Christianity*
1704  Death of Locke

## *Political turmoil in England*

Because of his association with Shaftesbury, Locke held several posts, but his public career ended with the fall of his patron. He then retired to his fellowship at Oxford. Because of poor health he spent the years 1675–80 in France. Locke was again associated with Shaftesbury on his return to England, but when Shaftesbury suffered further political reverses he was forced to flee to Holland. Locke also believed his own life might be in danger and went abroad. He was suspected of complicity in Monmouth's rebellion and was on the wanted list. His name was cleared; nevertheless he lived abroad under a false name and only returned to England when William III was safely on the throne. He refused an ambassadorship, pleading ill-health, but did take employment as commissioner of trade, which required only occasional attendance in London. In 1691 he retired to Oates in Essex. He was a guest of the Masham family and died in 1704, while Lady Masham was reading the Psalms to him.

Locke's chief works are *Letters on Tolerance* (1689), an *Essay Concerning Human Understanding* (1690) and *Two Treatises of Civil Government* (1690). He also published *Some Thoughts Concerning Education* (1693) and *The Reasonableness of Christianity* in the same year.

## Thought

Thomas Hobbes (1588–1679), a slightly earlier political thinker, had considered that the life of a person living in a state of nature would be 'solitary, poor, nasty, brutish and short'. Locke, on the other hand, considered living in a state of nature to be social in character, though undeveloped and requiring completion: 'peace, goodwill, mutual assistance and preservation'. People were always subject to the law of reason, which teaches respect for the life and property of another. War and violence come when individuals and princes abandon this law. There is, however, no superior being or institution to interpret this law so all individuals must interpret it for themselves and this causes confusion.

### Natural rights

Locke argued that there are natural rights of 'life, liberty and estate'. These natural rights are what all individuals bring to society in their own person; they are prior to primitive society. That is to say that the rights of individuals come before the rights of society. Society did not create natural rights and therefore, except in certain circumstances, cannot regulate them.

Estate or property is defined as whatever individuals have mixed with their own labour. If they have cleared, enclosed and tilled land, it is theirs. In nature all property was held in common as each had the right to draw subsistence from nature. However, civil society invented the notion of property to smooth out the difficulties that might otherwise arise.

### A social contract

Locke held that the state came into existence through agreement between individuals. Each individual agreed to give up to the community the natural right to enforce the law of nature. This original 'contract' was between individuals. It involved surrendering individual rights to the social group and, by this means, creating a civil power that exercised those rights on behalf of and for the welfare and protection of all.

The civil power is the right to make laws with penalties; by this means it regulates and preserves property, using force sanctioned by the community to execute laws in a way which could not be done by individuals alone.

It is important to notice that this can only be done for the common good and that not all powers are thereby surrendered. The contract is not absolute, but is formed for a limited and particular purpose. The only rights surrendered are those for communal existence. The only purpose of the state is to preserve 'life, liberty and estate'. It follows as a law of reason that when a civil society has been formed the majority decision holds sway.

Thus one owes duties to a state and one receives benefits from a state. If things do not work out the contract may be revoked and the agreement of citizens is no longer binding.

This is of course a fiction. There never was an 'original contract'. This fiction serves as an explanatory and justifying myth. What is more, people could leave the contract and go and live elsewhere. On the other hand, whoever joins the commonwealth accepts the original contract. Locke is unclear what is actually in the contract: the agreement between individual citizens to form a community, or the agreement between citizens and government.

### The separation of powers

Locke's theory of government involved what is known as the 'separation of powers'. Government involves exercising power in three ways:

(1) Power is exercised when laws are made; this is now called the *legislative power*.
(2) Power is exercised when decisions based on law are carried out. This is called *executive power*. In Locke's day this was very limited: no more than the maintenance of order, financial management

and collection of taxes, the pursuit of the country's interests abroad (diplomacy) and the waging of war. Nowadays it involves much more: health, welfare, education, the regulation of economic and commercial activity, agriculture, foreign trade, marine resources, industrial matters, environmental protection, transport and so on.

(3) Finally, there is *judicial power*. This is exercised when there are courts set up to judge and decide on differences between individuals and corporate bodies.

Locke's theory was that these three forms of power – legislative, executive and judicial – should never all be in the same hands.

In most Western democracies judicial power is quite independent of executive and legislative power. The border between executive and legislative power is less clear as most parliamentary democracies can only function if the government controls parliament. The distinction is probably clearest in the USA.

For Locke, society and government are distinct. Government exists for the well-being of society. If government betrays its trust it can and should be changed. When executive power, be it king or parliamentary government, becomes oppressive, power returns to the people who must provide alternative government.

## Appraisal

Locke's political theory remains somewhat vague. He tended to assume that the best practice of his day was sound. Moreover, he made very little effort to give a realistic analysis of the social contract; it remains artificial in appearance, though people today might say it has value as a foundational myth\*. Does the idea of a social

---

\* The word 'myth' is nowadays used in the sense of untrue or fictitious. Originally it meant tale or legend, and in pre-literate societies they told stories to explain why things were as they were. So 'myth' had an important explanatory or 'truth' function.

contract help your understanding of what it is to be a citizen in a modern liberal democracy? What are the consequences that flow from it?

Locke also failed to give much attention to the notion of the consent of the governed, or how the common will might best be consulted and expressed (e.g., modes of elections; who can be said to express the common will and for how long).

In addition, Locke's notion of all individuals retaining their basic freedom and consenting to hand over a portion of it to the government for the greater good was expressive of reality (for some people) at that time. In Locke's day one could opt out of the social contract, take oneself off to America and live more or less in total freedom in the wilderness. Is this possible today? Where would you go? And, what is more, would it be considered permissible?

Locke had no notion of minority rights, or of the duty of the community at large to be aware of them, to be sensitive to them and to move to accommodate them in the broadest sense. Such an expression of the importance of minority rights would be the work of John Stuart Mill in the nineteenth century.

Locke gave no thought to the common good. He supposed that the protection of private property and the common good are the same. Try to make a list of other components of the common good which seem important and valid to you.

Locke did, however, give people much to think about, and the gradual emergence of the modern liberal state owes much to his ideas. During his lifetime Locke was generally understood by his contemporaries and his ideas warmly welcomed. He lived at a time of vigorous political change when his country was seeking to limit the power of the monarch, set up regular parliaments, get rid of the worst elements of authoritarianism and establish limited religious freedom. Locke very much personified these aspirations.

# Charles-Louis de Secondat, Baron de Montesquieu

## Life

Montesquieu was born in La Brède castle, south of Bordeaux, in 1689. His father was a cavalry captain and a member of the minor nobility; his uncle was a successful lawyer. This was the career that Montesquieu was to follow. After rigorous studies he was himself to have a successful law career, but this was not the sum of his interests. His interest in the procedures of law was slight and he gradually became more interested in experimental research. He founded a prize for anatomy studies at the Academy of Bordeaux and he himself presented papers on the functioning of glands, on echoes, on weight and similar subjects.

He became famous when he published anonymously, in Amsterdam, a work called the *Persian Letters* (1721) in which he criticized contemporary French life and the absolutist and highly centralized monarchy, with its rigorous censorship. The work took the form of letters sent by Persian visitors in which they explain to their Persian readers what life is like in France. The opportunity for malicious and witty social comment was rarely missed.

Montesquieu also published works on the history and philosophy of law, with special emphasis on the principles of French constitutional thought, and he expressed an interest in the founding of a universal monarchy in Europe. In 1728 he was elected to the French Academy. He set out that year on a European tour, visiting Germany, Austria, Hungary, the Italian republics and Holland. He made a visit to England where he admired a constitution which guaranteed freedom; nevertheless he condemned the corruption of the parliamentary system.

Returning home, Montesquieu settled down to write a great work on the nature of law and on how laws should work together. This entailed a prodigious amount of reading. Montesquieu was to devote himself to this work for the last twenty years of his life, abandoning parlement, the Academy and the social round of the fashionable salons.

The *Spirit of the Laws* (*L'Esprit des lois*) was published in Geneva in 1748, in 31 volumes. By now Montesquieu had worn himself out. His eyesight in particular had been damaged by so much reading, and his general health was never to recover. He died in Paris in 1755.

---

### Timeline

1661  Beginning of the personal reign of Louis XIV
1671  Philosophy of Descartes banned in Paris
1673  Louis XIV restricts powers of the parlements (judicial bodies which registered or requested correction of the king's laws)
1689  Birth of Montesquieu
       Peter the Great rules in Russia
1690  Locke's *Two Treatises of Civil Government*
1721  Montesquieu publishes *Persian Letters*
1723  Abolition of the Royal Council; official majority of Louis XV
1728  Montesquieu elected to the French Academy; European tour
1738  Hume's *A Treatise of Human Nature*
1743  Reign of Louis XV
1748  Montesquieu publishes *The Spirit of the Laws*
1749  Imprisonment of Diderot
1750  Voltaire at the court of Frederick the Great; proposals for the *Encyclopaedia*
1751  The *Spirit of the Laws* placed on the Index
1753  Parlement exiled from Paris
1755  Death of Montesquieu

---

Witty and frivolous, sceptical and even cynical, Montesquieu gradually became more serene, understanding and optimistic. He had a universal curiosity, and huge syntheses were painfully constructed with much effort. His ideas are precise and lucid. In all things, Montesquieu displayed a highly developed sense of justice, concern for human

the environment in which it is to operate. Is there anything to be said for such a stance?

Montesquieu also suggests that any given government is imperfect, but that it has behind it an ideal that is an inspiration towards virtuous government.

Montesquieu's law of liberty is that 'Liberty is a right of doing whatever the law permits'. This probably means that if the law permits you to do something you will not be prevented from doing it and you will not be forced to act in a particular way when the law gives you freedom of scope.

The idea of 'separation of powers' which Montesquieu thought he saw working in England was probably not in fact the working-out of principle, it was the gradual evolution of practice over time. Montesquieu's own contribution to theory was his notion of 'balance'. This eventually became important both in the USA and in France; the notion of checks and balances is recognized in the US constitution (1787) and in the Declaration of the Rights of Man (1789).

# 7 Benedict de Spinoza: Rigorous Thought and Severe Conclusions

Spinoza has been described as both a hideous atheist and as a God-intoxicated man: obviously he cannot be both. He was in fact a rational pantheist who tried to construct a totally inclusive system, accounting for God, nature and human beings, by working from a single spiritual reality. His arguments were rigorously worked out and systematically built up, rather like one of Euclid's theorems.

Every age produces thinkers excited by the prospect of a complex philosophical structure meticulously and demonstrably worked out from a simple initial premise. Spinoza occupies a special place in the affections of such people.

Just before Spinoza was born, Holland had adopted the principle of freedom of thought. That small country was now a sanctuary for all those who were persecuted for their beliefs or speculations. In addition there was now at least one place where radical thinkers could get their books published. Spinoza, amongst others, took advantage of this newly proclaimed freedom.

## Life

Benedict de Spinoza was born in 1632. He was a philosopher, mathematician and scientist. He lived in an age when the explosion of knowledge had not yet made narrow specialization necessary, and all serious students could range over a wide variety of disciplines.

Spinoza was born in Amsterdam, his parents having fled there from Portugal in order to escape the Inquisition. He was given the education normal for a Jewish boy of his time. He studied the work of many Jewish thinkers and was strongly influenced by the medieval Jewish philosopher, theologian and medical scholar Moses Maimonides, who had tried to integrate faith and reason and bring Jewish thought closer to the system of Aristotle. Spinoza also had some knowledge of the Cabbala. However, he was soon accused of heresy and expelled from the synagogue at the age of 24. From then on he earned his living as a humble polisher of lenses. His friends tended to be radical Protestants. His first language appears to have been Spanish; he early learned Portuguese, then Latin and Greek. He was also acquainted with French, Italian, Hebrew and Dutch.

In 1660 Spinoza went to live in Leyden, moving in 1663 to The Hague. He first started writing a *Treatise on the Correction of the Understanding*, which was influenced by Descartes. (It was, however, also critical of Cartesian thought.) He next set out to write his major work, *Ethics*, yet he put this aside to write a book on the freedom of thought and action. He published this anonymously. Holland was, as we have noted, a relatively liberal place, free from the censorship pervasive elsewhere in Europe. Spinoza's book, however, shocked even Dutch opinion; it was widely attacked and he decided not to publish any more. He completed his *Ethics* and started work on a *Treatise on Politics*, which was unfinished when he died. In 1673 he was offered a post as Professor of Philosophy in Heidelberg, but he refused it on the grounds that he wished to keep complete freedom of thought and expression.

Spinoza's books were written in Latin. His work is rigorously logical and laid out like a series of geometry theorems, *more geometrico demonstratae* says one of his long titles. There are axioms succeeded by numbered propositions, often ending up with the letters QED.[*] This makes it quite difficult to read. However, his work aims to free human beings from all types of servitude of the mind and to promote the joy which comes from knowledge. There are three types of knowledge: faith, reason and rational intuition. For Spinoza, life in community is the coming together of beings who are accepted.

Spinoza is the complete rationalist; the severe features of his philosophical work follow from that quality of his thought.

---

[*]  *Quod erat demonstrandum:* which was to be demonstrated.

In spite of the serious and rigorous nature of his writing, Spinoza did have a human side and once wrote: 'There cannot be too much merriment, it is always good; on the other hand, melancholy is always bad.'

Spinoza never married. He died in 1677, at the age of 45, of tuberculosis.

---

**Timeline**

1632  Birth of Spinoza

1637  Descartes' *Discourse on Method*

1638  Galileo's Law on the movement of the pendulum

1649  Execution of Charles I of England

1651  Hobbes' *Leviathan*

1656  Spinoza expelled from the synagogue

1667  Milton's *Paradise Lost*

1670  Publication of Spinoza's *Treatise on Theology and Politics*

1677  Death of Spinoza; publication of his *Treatise on the Correction of the Understanding*; publication of his *Ethics*

---

## Thought

### *Spinoza's political thought*

Spinoza's *Treatise on Theology and Politics* is a blend of biblical criticism and political theory. He is the grandfather of modern, liberal biblical criticism, which really only took off in the nineteenth century.

His political thought was influenced by Hobbes, who taught that in a state of nature there is no law. Wrong is a question of disobeying the law and, says Spinoza, because there is no law in a state of nature, there can be no right or wrong. Spinoza believed that the monarch can do no wrong, (which seems a little strange; all he had to do was look around him) and that the Church should be subordinate to the state. He condemned rebellion, but did not think that subjects should sacrifice all their rights to the monarch. It is difficult to say if Spinoza believed that rights properly come from the law or whether they come from some form of natural law.

What is the difference between **law** and **natural law**? Law is a set of rules that have been debated, decided and promulgated; they can be changed. Natural law is something more important, fundamental and given than the law and the will of the monarch. We say that natural law is prior to positive law. It is not within the powers of human beings to change it.

The **Cabbala** is a collection of writings on the occult science of communication with the supernatural world.

**Finite** means limited, kept within boundaries.

**Substance** nowadays means a form of material, like earth or lead or wool. In metaphysics it is a concept referring to the essence or form that makes matter what it is. The substance of a stool makes the wood a stool rather than a walking stick.

**Metaphysics** is the study of being as being; speculation about the meaning of what is; the study of first principles and first causes; the rational knowledge of those realities that go beyond us; the rational study of things in themselves.

**Pantheism** is the religious and philosophical view that God and the world are the same.

**Logical necessity** decides what must inevitably exist or occur; invariable logical laws or requirements dictate what must be.

**Materialism** is the philosophical view that physical matter is the only reality and that all thought, feeling, mind or will may be explained in terms of that physical reality.

**Determinism** is the philosophical teaching that every event, act or decision is the inevitable result of what has happened beforehand and that human will can play no part in altering this.

*Spinoza's metaphysics*

Spinoza held that there was only one substance: 'God or Nature'. Nothing that is finite can be its own substance. Mind and matter, thought and extension, are attributes of God. God has an infinite number of other attributes, but we cannot know them. Souls and objects are not things; they are aspects of God's being (they are adjectives rather than nouns). Immortality involves becoming more and more part of divine being; it is quite impersonal, we do not retain individual identity.

God is a single unified substance and that substance is self-determined, it cannot be explained by other causes outside itself: there is nothing outside itself to make it what it is. When we think of this substance in terms of nature, we think in terms of physical properties and extension (it takes up space). When we think about substance in terms of God, we think in terms of thought. Spinoza's opinion was that the two attributes of 'God or Nature' are extension and thought. However, normally when ordinary human beings think about mind we do not in fact think of it in terms of body or vice versa.

According to Spinoza, substance takes different forms, which he calls 'modes'. Modes need to be explained in terms of something else. They are explicable in terms of substance. It might help to think of modes in terms of bubbles in lemonade. You can have the liquid (substance) without the bubbles, but you can't have the bubbles (modes) without the liquid. That is the way substance is necessary for modes. Inanimate objects, plants and animals (including humans) are all modes. That is why things change. Since we are modes we are part of substance. Substance predetermines the modes.

Spinoza held that everything turns out the way that it must turn out. Substance, which is God or nature, shapes itself as thought and extension. Spinoza taught that everything is governed by total logical necessity. In the sphere of the mind there is no free will. In the sphere of physical matter there is no chance. Spinoza held that there is no afterlife and no immortal soul.

Everything that happens comes about as a result of God's nature: it is logically impossible for the world or events to be other than the way they are. That was what Spinoza meant when he said that the world is the best of all possible worlds. If we see something as sinful, this is only so because what is negative is bad. What is negative only exists from the point of view of finite creatures. There is nothing negative in God.

Finite things are defined by what they are not. 'All determination is negation', said Spinoza. A rather crude way of understanding this is to think of a hole. The hole is defined by its boundaries: you do not see it; all you see is the outline of the surrounding earth. A hole is something that isn't there. Only God is wholly positive, and God must be absolutely infinite. This suggests that everything that exists is God or part of God. For this reason Spinoza has been seen as a pantheist.

Spinoza's physics, his thinking about what is, was materialistic and deterministic. Yet within this framework he tried to find a place for reverence and devotion to what is good.

## The passions

Spinoza's view of psychology was egoistic: individuals serve self. Self-preservation is the basic underlying cause of the passions; it governs all human behaviour. There are occasional exceptions: for instance, love can overcome hatred. Feelings are called passions when they arise out of inadequate ideas and when we are ourselves subject to the power of outside forces. A feeling ceases to be a passion as soon as we form a clear and distinct idea of it. What is real and positive in us unites us to the whole; when this happens self-preservation changes its nature.

## Spinoza's ethical thought

Spinoza taught that the mind's highest good is the knowledge of God; its highest virtue is to know God. If individuals are wise that is what they will seek as their goal.

What happens to us is determined by outside causes and because we are unwilling parts of the larger whole (i.e., universal nature). We are free in so far as we have, through understanding, sought and succeeded in grasping the reality of the whole. But Spinoza denied that human beings have free will in the true sense.

Spinoza believed that all wrongdoing was the result of intellectual error. In this he agreed with Socrates. All emotions have to do with either time past or time future. But, for Spinoza, time is unreal; consequently emotions are contrary to reason. The wise person will seek to see the world as God sees it, '*sub specie aeternitatis*' (from the viewpoint of eternity). The future is unalterable, as is the past. It is unwise to view the future as uncertain; such a mistaken outlook produces both hope and fear.

Spinoza wanted to free human beings from fear. He objected to emotions that are passions, those that spring from inadequate ideas. Wisdom, however, is the intellectual love of God and that is a union of both thought and emotion: true thought together with joy because one is grasping truth (i.e., the understanding that everything is part of God). We may love God, but should not expect that God might love us in return: a deity who loved would not be divine; God is not affected by any pleasure (or pain).

However, even though he aimed at what he called 'intellectual love of God', Spinoza was not a religious mystic.

---

### *Ethics* (1677)

- If something is the cause of itself then it exists necessarily.
- Substance alone is self-caused, infinite and free. God is the only substance.
- God necessarily exists. God is possessed of infinite attributes.
- We know only two of God's infinite attributes, which are thought and extension.
- Thought and extension are characteristics of the same substance, therefore whatever happens to body happens to mind; it is another phase of the same event.

- A false idea is an idea which is improperly related to God. When we achieve adequate ideas we become adequate causes of the body's modifications; we then possess human freedom, which is freedom from human enslavement to the passions.
- Knowledge of God is the greatest virtue of the mind.

## Spinoza's theory of knowledge

In his *Treatise on the Correction of the Understanding* Spinoza held that there are four levels of knowledge:

(1) Hearsay: the testimony of others.
(2) Perception of knowledge from vague or confused experience: I know that in certain situations such and such is likely to happen to me for I have known it to happen to others.
(3) The essence of one thing inferred from the essence of another, but not adequately.
(4) The thing itself perceived through its essence or through knowledge of its proximate cause.

In his *Ethics* Spinoza talked of three types of knowledge.

(1) The *level of opinion or imagination*. This does not spring from the active power of the mind, but reflects changes and states produced by other bodies. It reflects experience, but is vague.
(2) The *level of reason*. All minds, which are ideas of bodies, reflect on the common properties of bodies: motion, weight, solidity, etc. We apply logic to the understanding of things and deduce a system of general propositions. Knowledge of this kind is necessarily true.
(3) *Intuitive knowledge*. At this third level the mind returns to individual things and perceives them in their essential relation to God and not as isolated phenomena.

*Freedom and servitude*

Spinoza taught that we live in servitude of the mind when we lack the power to moderate and check emotions. Desires arise from passive emotions. (Remember they focus on self-preservation and arise out of inadequate ideas, particularly when we are ourselves subject to the power of outside forces.) From passive emotions we derive our knowledge of good and evil. However, it is possible to possess the positive knowledge that leads us to reach the ideal yet at the same time to do bad deeds.

So we live this life of servitude to passive emotions. Set against it is the life of reason, which is a life of virtue. If we act under the guidance of reason we act virtuously. To understand is to be free, no longer enslaved by the emotions. Hatred depends on the fact that we do not recognize that all human beings are similar and have a common good. When we come to understand that, we then stop wishing evil on fellow human beings.

## Appraisal

Spinoza has been seen as the most honourable, most virtuous and most lovable of the great philosophers. He was a man of noble ethical outlook. Philosophy and religion were one and the same to him and he lived out this conviction. He had no thought for fame or riches; he earned his living frugally.

However, Spinoza's belief that all events are equally the result of logical necessity cannot be squared with modern logic and scientific method. Facts are discovered by observation, not by reflection. When we make correct inferences about what will happen we do so because we have built up a body of observable data and not because some impersonal logical force is operating.

Spinoza is often held to be a forerunner of the modern scientific outlook, in that he tried to give a naturalistic explanation for events and did not seek to explain them in terms of how they lead towards the fulfilment of a 'grand plan', what is called final cause. Be that as it may, the method required for scientific research (the empirical investigation of phenomena) is not the method Spinoza used in his philosophy.

Spinoza's ethics try to show us how to live nobly even when we come to accept the narrow limits of human power. Spinoza held that one should not entertain worry or fear with regard to misfortune or death; but while we can serenely overcome dread with regard to ourselves, our very humanity dictates that we feel these emotions on behalf of those whom we love.

Are calamities merely passing discords which will make us more appreciative of a final, ultimate harmony? Is it comforting to think that human life is a tiny part of the life of the universe?

It is unlikely that Spinoza's main aim was to establish a theory of knowledge or propose a theory of government. Rather, he sought a way of achieving proper peace of mind and freedom from servitude to the passions. What do you think of Spinoza's idea of freedom as the release from passion which the wise man attains once he views all things from the standpoint of eternity?

Spinoza focused on the larger picture rather than being preoccupied with individual pain. There are times when this can be a helpful corrective to self-absorption.

The possibility of a comprehensive system which accounts for God and humanity in terms of a sole spiritual reality continued to intrigue thinkers for hundreds of years; it may not be dead yet. Are there other thinkers described in this book who sought to construct an all-embracing system on the basis of a single principle?

# 8 David Hume: Empirical Verification

How do you know it's raining? You look out the window. How do you know the traffic is going to be heavy on the way to work? You listen to the radio traffic report. How do they know? They have people out there checking it out. If there's a change they will tell you. How will they know there's a change? They observe.

Just common sense, you might say: But for a long time such a way of going about things was considered an inferior way of knowing. A person who lived by such trial and error was called 'a vulgar empiric'. Nowadays such ways of knowing are considered by some to be the only route to knowledge. Only facts gleaned by such a method may be properly called knowledge. How did it all change? We have to give the credit (or blame) to David Hume.

## Life

David Hume was born in Edinburgh, where he lived for much of his life. He did, however, spend long stints working and studying abroad, mainly in France, where he met many of the figures of the French Enlightenment. His family tried to turn him into a lawyer, but he was more interested in literature, 'philosophy and general learning'. However, he had to earn a living and so he went into business in Bristol. He wasn't very good at it, so he gave it up and went to France, where he decided he would devote himself to literature and live a frugal life, given that he had no money. He composed his most famous work, *A Treatise of Human Nature*, in France, during 1734–37. To his great disappointment it 'fell dead-born from the press', causing not 'a murmur among the zealots'. The young Hume had hoped that his book would be bitterly attacked, particularly by religious conservatives. He had planned to meet such attacks with stinging retorts, but nobody reacted.

From 1737 to 1746 Hume lived at home with his mother, brother and sister. He wrote and published *Essays, Moral and Political.* This book was more successful than his first effort and he was so heartened by this that he set about rewriting the first book, hoping it would get a better reception than before.

Hume applied for the professorship of ethics at the University of Edinburgh, but his candidacy was effectively blocked, probably because he was reputed to be an atheist. He worked for a while as a private tutor, then abroad as a personal secretary. His revision of his first work continued and was published piecemeal under a different title (which it generally carries today): *An Enquiry Concerning Human Understanding.* In 1751 *An Enquiry Concerning the Principles of Morals* was published. This was a rewriting of the third part of his *Treatise. Political Discourses* appeared the following year. Hume's reputation was now assured.

In 1752 Hume became librarian to the Faculty of Advocates in Edinburgh, and he and his sister set up house together in the city. He now took up the writing of English history. From 1763 to 1766 he was secretary to the British embassy in Paris. Here he moved in circles connected with the group known as the Encyclopedists. When he returned to London he brought the great Jean-Jacques Rousseau with him, but Rousseau was impossible to get on with and the experiment did not last long. During 1767–69 Hume enjoyed a brief political career in London, but he returned to Edinburgh where he died in 1776. His *Dialogues Concerning Natural Religion* was published after his death.

In his autobiography Hume describes himself as of 'mild disposition, of command of temper, of an open, social and cheerful humour, capable of attachment, but little susceptible of enmity, and of great moderation in all my passions. Even my love of literary fame, my ruling passion, never soured my temper, notwithstanding my frequent disappointments.' He was apparently quite plump, like 'a turtle-eating Alderman'. He spoke English with a broad Scots accent and his French accent was deemed inadequate.

Edinburgh in Hume's lifetime was undergoing something of

a renaissance. The new town had been rebuilt with wide elegant streets and finely proportioned, if somewhat severe, buildings. (You may still admire the city that Hume knew, as it is largely unspoiled today.) Hume lived in the old town, where there is a statue of him looking across at his house.

Hume was one of the leading figures of the Scottish Enlightenment, a period of renovation, mental vigour and learning in eighteenth-century Scotland.

---

**The Enlightenment** was a period in European history covering roughly the eighteenth century. It was marked by the rejection of old authorities (such as the Church), the adoption of freedom and the appeal to reason in matters of belief and conduct. 'Enlightened Despots' ruled in several European countries and Enlightenment ideals were highly influential in the framing of the constitution of the USA.

**The Encyclopedists** were a group of Frenchmen who were major players in the Enlightenment. They set out to make the sum of rational knowledge available in accessible form to ordinary readers. Their work was called the *Encyclopedia, or Critical Dictionary of Sciences, Arts and Trades*.* Major importance was given to the technical application of knowledge, and practical specialists such as engineers and doctors were consulted. The *Encyclopedia* ran to 35 volumes, and was fiercely opposed by the clergy and the nobility. Its success was due to the business acumen of the bookseller Le Breton and the energy of Diderot.

---

## Thought

Hume developed empirical theory to its logical conclusion and, according to Bertrand Russell, 'by making it self-consistent made it incredible'. Empirical philosophy places great emphasis on what we perceive (i.e., the information we obtain by our senses).

* *Encyclopédie, on Dictionnaire raisonné des sciences, des arts et des métiers* (Paris: Le Breton, 1751–76).

## Timeline

1707  Act of Union between Engla

1711  Birth of David Hume

1727  George II King of Great Britain and

1738–40  Publication of Hume's *A Treatise o*

1741–42 Publication of Hume's *Essays, Moral an*

1742  Handel's *Messiah*

1751–76  Publication of Diderot's (*et al.*) *Encyclopedia*

1751  Hume's *Treatise of Human Nature* becomes *An Enqu*
        *Concerning Human Understanding*

1752  Publication of Hume's *Political Discourses*

1756–61  Gradual publication of Hume's *History of England*

1760  Accession of George III

1763–66  Hume appointed Secretary to British Embassy in Paris

1767–69  Hume in London, as Undersecretary of State

1769  Returns to Edinburgh

1774  Louis XVI King of France

1775–83  American War of Independence

1776  Death of Hume

Hume endeavoured to bring the experimental method of reasoning into moral subjects such as ethics and the social sciences. He hoped that he would be able to discover the limits of human knowledge in mathematics, physics and the social sciences. He thought it was possible to discover general laws concerning human thinking and behaviour.

### Impressions and ideas

Hume identified two types of perception: impressions and ideas.

- Impressions have great force and vividness.
- Ideas are faint echoes of those impressions in thinking and reasoning.

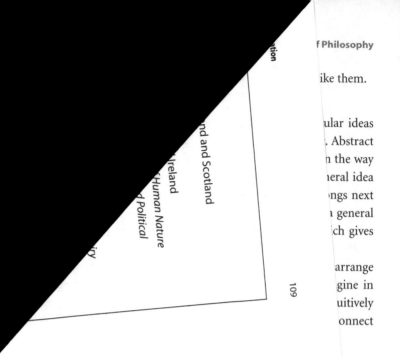

ike them.

ular ideas
. Abstract
n the way
eral idea
ngs next
a general
ch gives

arrange
gine in
uitively
onnect

...*Nature* (1739)

- All our knowledge comes from impressions and ideas. Impressions are more forceful than ideas.
- We preserve and arrange ideas using memory and imagination.
- We have only ideas of particular things which we come to consider collectively by the use of general terms. We have no abstract, general ideas.
- We gain certainty from the intuitive recognition of similarities or differences in ideas.
- We also connect a series of intuitions, e.g. in mathematics.
- Through observation we form the habit of expecting events of one kind to follow events of another kind. This is the basis of our knowledge of causal relationships, but all we observe is that the events are conjoined. We observe no necessary relationship between them.
- We should be sceptical of all conclusions reached by the use of reason or on the basis of sense experience.

## Knowledge and probability

The most important part of Hume's work came when he dealt with knowledge and probability. Probability is uncertain knowledge that comes from empirical information by means of chains of reasoning that are not demonstrative. Everything except direct observation, logic and mathematics falls into this category. Hume was very unwilling to accept 'probable' knowledge.

Hume maintained there are seven kinds of philosophical relation. Some of these depend only on the ideas, and therefore they give certain knowledge: resemblance, contrariety, degrees in quality and proportion in quantity or number. The other philosophical relations can be changed without any change in the ideas, and these give only probable knowledge. They are identity, space–time relations and causality.

## Causation

We see the full force of Hume's philosophy – and also why its self-consistency made it hard to believe – in Hume's thoughts about cause.

In Aristotle, the scholastics and in Descartes, the connection of cause and effect was considered to be necessary in exactly the same way as logical connections are necessary. Modern ideas of causation come from David Hume. We can, said Hume, only know cause and effect from experience, not from reasoning or reflection.

When you kick a football, you cause it to travel a certain distance, hopefully in the direction of the goal. Do you see your foot causing the ball to travel? You do not, Hume would say. What you see is not causation. You see two different things, one following after the other:

1. The foot kicks the ball.
2. The ball travels towards the goal.

You perceive only ideas that are together and following one after the other. You feel there is more to the sequence than that. But what evidence have you for that 'more'? If you do not perceive a necessary connection, why do you believe in a cause?

The notion of cause is not intuitively obvious; what is more, it cannot be demonstrated. When we think about events we don't see them as cause and we don't necessarily think of them in terms of their causes. If events can be thought of as uncaused it is possible that they occur uncaused.

To go further: why should particular causes have particular effects? Our causal reasoning is made up of impressions of sense and of memory. We imagine that two events are related with an unknown connection between them. But, Hume would argue, there is no reason to think of one effect and not another when a 'cause' occurs.

Is experience responsible for this assumption of 'cause'? If reason is involved we have to assume that there is a principle at work here: the principle of the uniformity of nature. The principle of the uniformity of nature is one of the postulates of modern science. That is to say it is assumed always to be operating. But, Hume would again say, there is no evidence for it!

Hume argued that we have reason to be sceptical about all conclusions reached by the use of reason.

---

**Perception** is our awareness of sensations coming through the sense organs: sight, touch, smell, hearing and taste.

**Scepticism**, in its extreme form, is a philosophical outlook intent upon demonstrating methodically that the human person cannot attain certainty or knowledge. It is a refusal to admit that knowledge in matters of absolute truth or religious teaching can be reached. The word popularly refers to a refusal of religious commitment because of doubts over the existence of God.

**Metaphysics** is the study of being as being; speculation about the meaning of what is; the study of first principles and first causes; the rational knowledge of those realities that go beyond us; the rational study of things in themselves.

A **postulate** is an element, belief or principle that is necessary in order for reason to function; a fundamental element, a basic principle; what is assumed without proof as self-evident or generally accepted; what is necessary for an argument; an axiom, a requirement, a prerequisite.

*There is no such thing as the self*

Hume claimed that he had no impression of the self. By his doctrine therefore, he could have no idea of the self. He was aware of impressions and therefore, of ideas. But whenever he tried to catch an impression of himself without an idea he failed. All he could grasp were the ideas, many of them, all quickly succeeding each other; but he could never get an impression of self. The self was never perceived; therefore we can have no idea of it. Strictly speaking, this is not a denial of the self, it means rather that we cannot know if there is a self or not. Hume's ideas have frequently been used to claim that there is no such thing as metaphysics; it is a delusion.

This banishes the last vestiges of 'substance' from Western philosophy. Other philosophers had attacked the notion (Berkeley, for instance); Hume finally got rid of it. Many believe that doing without the notion of the self also abolishes the notion of the soul in theology and, indeed, that it is not necessary to make a distinction between subject and object when one is analysing knowledge.

*What is empiricism?*

Empiricism is a principle which refuses to accept any ready-given *a priori* knowledge (things that are necessarily true or necessarily false). It is the notion that all our knowledge comes by means of our sense-organs (touch, taste, smell, hearing, sight), from experience. Things are true because they happen to be true and we know them to be so by observation.

Appraisal

Hume appears to have started his philosophical investigations believing that scientific method leads us to truth. He appears to have ended them believing that 'knowledge' is never rational and so we know nothing. Total scepticism is not self-consistent. If one doubts

## Logic and scientific method

When we reason and acquire knowledge we make use of a number of devices and principles. Here is very brief summary of some of the important ones:

*The laws of thought:* There are three laws of thought:

- The law of identity: x is x.
- The law of non-contradiction: nothing can be both x and not-x.
- The law of excluded middle: everything is either x or not-x.

These three laws have to do with identifying what you are talking about and what you are saying about it. They seem obvious; no thinking can happen without using them. They are extremely difficult to prove without at some stage assuming them to be true.

*The principles of deduction:* These are the principles involved in deducing conclusions from already established facts. If the premises are true and the inference valid, the conclusion must be true.

*The principle of induction:* This is the process of establishing probable information on the basis of observed regularities. (Hume was extremely sceptical of the possibility of doing this.)

*The postulate of the uniformity of nature:* This is the assumption that the elements of nature always act in a regular fashion as if following laws.

*The postulate of universal causation:* This is the assumption that for every event in the universe there was before it a set of conditions that inevitably caused it to happen.

*Evaluating scientific explanations:* When we think we have made a discovery we put it forward as a hypothesis. This means we are tentatively proposing it as true and that it has to be evaluated. We judge it using these criteria:

*Relevance:* The hypothesis must explain a precisely defined fact.

*Testability:* There must be the possibility of making an observation that will confirm whether the hypothesis is true or false. And this test must be capable of being repeated.

> *Compatibility:* The hypothesis must be consistent with other well-established facts or theories.
>
> *Predictive or explanatory power:* The hypothesis must allow us to predict something that we will be able to observe. Or it must allow us to explain something that wasn't understood up to now.
>
> *Simplicity:* If two hypotheses satisfy all the other criteria, the simplest one that explains all the facts is the one that will be accepted.
>
> It will be seen from our survey of all these points that new knowledge is not always a question of inevitable deductions but hesitant and probable conclusions. What is more, we use a huge range of principles and devices that are themselves assumed or adopted cautiously.

everything one has to doubt the worth of one's argument in arriving at that conclusion. Therefore one cannot believe the conclusion that one knows nothing.

If the principle of induction is true, then we can claim to be correct when we say there is universal causation and that like causes have like effects. If the principle of induction is not true, then we have to be sceptical about all empirical knowledge.

Why is this? Because when we say we observe uniformities in the world we assume patterns and say that we can argue from them towards a case for probable inference. But we have already assumed the principle of induction before we have proved it. And we don't seem to be able to prove it without using it. This is called circular argument.

Hume rejected the principle of induction. But without the principle of induction modern science is impossible.

Hume seems to have set his sights too high or restricted his vision too narrowly when he reduced all knowledge to what can be directly observed. It caused him to reject tools which we regularly use in our explorations and which regularly work and allow us to make discoveries.

In assessing the validity of Hume's empirical philosophy, you might like to consider the following questions:

- What sort of knowledge comes from direct observation?
- What sort of knowledge requires more than direct observation?
- Where might inductive processes be valuable?
- What is the value of deduction?
- How might one use deductive arguments with tentative hypotheses?

After Hume, what was needed was a justification of induction, the logic of scientific enquiry and the philosophy of science. Many have tackled the problems, yet Hume's arguments frequently return with force.

# 9 Immanuel Kant: the Critique of Reason

The leading philosophers of the eighteenth century were the British empiricists: Locke, Berkeley and Hume. They were socially aware and of kind, generous and gentle outlook. Nonetheless, the principal trend of their thought led to subjectivism. It was the agnostic, and eventually the sceptical, outlook of David Hume that woke Kant from his 'dogmatic slumbers' and spurred him to think afresh about almost all the problems of knowledge. His work was produced at a time when there was tension between the continental insistence on rational thought and the British emphasis on sense experience. His work is difficult to understand and systematize. Many consider him the greatest of modern philosophers. German Idealism had its greatest influence following, and influenced by, Kant.

Immanuel Kant

## Life

Kant led a somewhat humdrum, undramatic life. He was born in 1724 in Königsberg (Kaliningrad), in eastern Prussia, where his father worked as a saddler. Kant was brought up in the devout tradition of pietism: a religious reform movement which wanted to renew the devotional tradition of Lutheran spirituality. To the end of his life he appreciated sincere religious practice.

Kant remained in his home town for both his secondary and university education. At university he was much influenced by his professor of logic and metaphysics. Because of him, Kant also developed an interest in modern science (i.e., in the theories of Newton). He first earned his living as a private tutor, gained his doctorate and then set up as a lecturer.

Kant was later to call these years his pre-critical period. During this time he lectured frequently on a wide variety of subjects: logic, physics, metaphysics, morals, mathematics, anthropology, education, geography and mineralogy. Some fifteen years later, in 1770, he was appointed professor of logic at Königsberg. The usual system of university teaching at the time was for a professor and his students to follow a set textbook: the teacher commented on the book as the class progressed. Kant's lectures are known to have been traditional in this fashion, though he was critical of his texts and was reputed to have a certain dry sense of humour. He was convinced that students needed factual knowledge as well as the ability to think for themselves.

Kant was not widely travelled; indeed, he rarely ventured beyond his home area. He did, however, have wide interests, and he enjoyed going out into society and meeting those who had travelled abroad. He was noted as being a man of very fixed routine and fussy punctuality. We do not know exactly when his precritical period ended. His new critical stage is supposed to date from his appointment as professor, but his first major work, the *Critique of Pure Reason*, was not published for another eleven years (in 1781). Further works followed. He continued to lecture on many subjects and to write freely.

To get through this enormous programme Kant had to be very disciplined with his time. His daily routine was (and still is) famous. He got up before five o'clock in the morning and spent the hour from five to six drinking tea, smoking a pipe and reflecting on the day ahead. He then spent an hour preparing his lecture. Summer and winter timetables differed so the lecture was either from seven to nine or from eight to ten. He then wrote for two hours. He enjoyed conversation and company at his midday meal, which often lasted two hours. Afterwards he took a walk, read until ten and then went to bed.

The Prussian emperor once took offence at Kant's views on scripture and Christian doctrine. Kant refused to retract them, but promised not to repeat such views in writings or lectures. When the emperor died, however, Kant considered himself released from the promise and published *The Conflict of the Faculties*, which discussed tensions between biblical belief and critical reason.

Kant was remembered as a sincere friend, and while careful with his money, he was generous to the needy. He was an earnest man, devoted to duty. He believed in God, but was not a regular churchgoer. His religious outlook was practical and centred around the notion of moral responsibility. He is said to have remarked that advance in moral goodness is accompanied by abandonment of prayer. He sympathized with the ideals of both the American and French Revolutions (at least until the Reign of Terror). He never married, and died in 1804.

---

### Timeline

1721  Peter the Great becomes Tsar of Russia
      Montesquieu's *Persian Letters*
1724  Birth of Immanuel Kant
1739  Hume's *Treatise of Human Nature*
1740  Kant enters the University of Königsberg
1751  First volume of Diderot's *Encyclopedia*
1755  Kant lectures at Königsberg (his precritical period)

1762  Rousseau's *Emile* and *The Social Contract*
1770  Kant appointed professor at Königsberg
1775  Beginning of the American War of Independence
1781  Publication of Kant's *Critique of Pure Reason*
1785  Kant's *Fundamental Principles of the Metaphysics of Morals*
1788  Kant publishes his *Critique of Practical Reason*
1789  Kant publishes his *Conflict of the Faculties*
       Declaration of the Rights of Man and the beginning of the
          French Revolution
1790  Kant's *Critique of Judgement*
1804  Death of Kant
       Napoleon crowned Emperor of the French

## Thought

**Idealism** is a philosophical outlook that subordinates all existence to thought. German Idealism of the eighteenth and nineteenth centuries had similarities to the Romantic movement. Idealists emphasize the critique of knowledge as a means of reaching philosophical conclusions; they stress mind as opposed to matter; they reject utilitarian ethics.

**Romanticism** was an intellectual, artistic, musical, poetic outlook of the late eighteenth and early nineteenth centuries in Europe. Individual feeling was more important than reason, the human imagination more important than the classical representations of human experience.

**Utilitarianism** is a philosophical doctrine which made the principle of utility (whatever promoted the greatest happiness of the greatest number) the rule of all individual and social action.

### Kant's theory of knowledge

Part of the aim of Kant's *Critique of Pure Reason* was to show that our knowledge does not all come from our experience; rather it is known *a priori*, because of the structure of our minds. The *a priori* is what is given before any experience comes into play.

There are two types of proposition (statement):

*Analytic propositions* are those where the meaning of the predicate is part of the meaning of the subject: 'Water is wet'. In this statement the notion that you get wet in water is part of what we mean by water, part of its definition: the predicate 'wet' is necessarily involved in the subject 'water'. Experience may back up *a priori* judgements, but their basis is not in experience.

*Synthetic propositions* are statements we make because we have come to know their contents through experience. 'When I was stung by a bee it was much more painful than a wasp sting.' Empirical propositions are known through sense experience.

Hume had shown that the law of causality is synthetic. Kant agreed, but claimed it was known *a priori*. Kant set out to show that synthetic *a priori* propositions are possible.

---

### *The Critique of Pure Reason* (1781)

It was essential to show that synthetic *a priori* truths are possible in order to establish metaphysics as a science. Synthetic *a priori* truths are universally and necessarily true (this is what *a priori* means), but we must show they are necessary by doing more than analysing the meanings of the statements expressing them (this is what synthetic means).

- Intuition and understanding are the two sources of knowledge.
- Space and time are the *a priori* forms of intuition. We cannot perceive anything unless we cast it mentally in terms of space and time.
- The categories of understanding are the *a priori* conditions of understanding.
- The categories of quantity are unity, plurality, totality.
- The categories of quality are reality, negation, limitation.

- The categories of relation are substance and accident; cause and effect; reciprocity between agent and patient.
- The categories of modality are possibility–impossibility; existence–non-existence; necessity–contingency.
- When we use the *a priori* forms of intuition together with the categories of understanding we perceive how it is possible to arrive at principles of knowledge. The presuppositions of science are synthetic *a priori*.
- In the area of theological speculation, we cannot, in the absence of empirical evidence, produce convincing arguments for the existence of God.

## The postulates of science

Are the presuppositions of science synthetic *a priori*? When we were examining the thought of David Hume we laid out a summary of the postulates of science pointing out that we use a huge range of principles and devices that are assumed or adopted cautiously. (See Chapter 8, pp. 114–15). Is Kant's description of those presuppositions of science as synthetic *a priori* helpful? Is it true that the way we go about acquiring scientific knowledge, methodology, is not itself given by experience but adopted because of the structure of our minds?

## Kant's theory of space and time

Kant regarded space and time as moulds into which we must mentally squeeze all objects if we are to experience them. We do not get the notion of space from experience; we already suppose it exists whenever we regard a sensation as coming from something outside of ourselves. We find it impossible to imagine that there could be no space. This is more than an abstract concept. There is only one space. 'Spaces' are parts of space, not instances of space.

Kant suggests that Euclidean geometry is known *a priori*: though it cannot be derived from logic alone (hence synthetic *a priori*).

Many have objected that time cannot be treated in this way. Subjective and objective time are identical.

---

**A postulate** is an element, belief or principle that is necessary in order for reason to function; a fundamental element, a basic principle; what is assumed without proof as self-evident or generally accepted; what is necessary for an argument; an axiom, a requirement, a prerequisite.

**Metaphysics** is the study of being as being; speculation about the meaning of what is; the study of first principles and first causes; the rational knowledge of those realities that go beyond us; the rational study of things in themselves.

**Categorical** means what is without exception or qualification, what is absolute and certain.

---

### The end of metaphysics?

The use of the categories comes into play when we apply them to things given in sense intuition. We cannot apply them to things-in-themselves. Applying the category 'substance' to things-in-themselves gives us no knowledge about them. We cannot use the principles of understanding to infer the existence of supersensible beings like God. This would suggest that metaphysics is pointless. But Kant seems to have regarded the impulse to metaphysics as a permanent urge of the human mind.

Two words associated with Kant are *noumenal* and *phenomenal.* The *noumenon* is what is known by the mind as opposed to the senses. Things in themselves are *noumena.* We cannot say they are there by intuition. We must say they have to be there to account for *phenomena,* which are the appearances we grasp through our senses.

### Kant's Copernican revolution in philosophy

Kant set out to solve the question: How are synthetic *a priori* propositions possible? He held that in all knowledge there is an *a priori* element. This element is contributed by the mind itself. Without this *a priori* element, knowledge is impossible.

The rationalist philosophers who came before Kant held that all knowledge is analytical and *a priori*. They were not concerned with observed facts. Empiricists held all knowledge to be synthetic and *a posteriori*. Kant rejected both these attitudes. He taught that knowledge is possible because it is structured under the forms of space and time and related by concepts like causality. These are the work of the knowing mind. In order to become objects of knowledge things must conform to the structure of the knowing mind.

*Practical reason*

Kant developed his thoughts about the practical use of reason in *The Critique of Practical Reason*. The central notion is that the moral law demands justice: happiness is proportional to virtue. Only providence can ensure this. Providence has not ensured it in this life. Therefore there must be a God and a future life. There must also be freedom, for without it there would be no such thing as virtue.

---

**The Critique of Practical Reason (1788)**

- We can only claim that morality is objective and universal if it is founded on pure reason.
- Moral laws are universal and categorical because of the form they take, not because of their content.
- The basic law of pure practical reason is to act in such a way that you would wish that what you were doing might become a universal law and to apply to all persons and situations.
- If we did not have the moral law we should never know we were free. For a human being, 'you ought to . . .' implies, 'you are able to . . .'
- The rational postulates of the practical reason are:
    The human being is free.
    The soul is immortal.
    God exists.

## *Kant on religion*

Kant makes it clear that he believes in God; nevertheless in a section of *The Critique of Pure Reason* he set out to refute the traditional arguments for the existence of God. Briefly, these (known as the theistic arguments) were the ontological argument of St Anselm of Canterbury and the five ways of St Thomas Aquinas (see Chapter 4, pp. 64–5). Kant refutes these ways of thinking about God in a series of arguments that are quite technical. Basically he says they simply repeat the ontological argument over and over again. His problem with the ontological argument is that it considers 'existence' to be a predicate.

Existence is considered to be a *quality*, like being tall, or rich, or kind. But he says a hundred thalers (coins) that I imagine have exactly the same qualities as a hundred real thalers. To put it another way, it is possible to say, 'Some tall men are well dressed'; but it makes no sense at all to say, 'Some tall men do not exist.' Therefore 'existence' is not at all like being 'well dressed'. Existence is not a predicate. Therefore the ontological argument is formally flawed.

Turning to the argument from contingency (the cosmological proof), Kant maintains it argues along the lines of: 'If anything exists then an Absolute Being exists. I exist therefore an Absolute Being exists.' This is the ontological argument all over again and must be rejected for those same reasons.

In considering the argument from design (the physico-theological proof), Kant treats the argument with respect but maintains it proves at best a designer and fails to reason to an adequate notion of God.

Kant refutes the traditional arguments as being mostly based on a flawed ontological argument, or as being inadequate to our conception of God. Instead, he puts forward a moral argument for the existence of God. Pure reason leads us to form three ideas: God, freedom and immortality. Reason leads us to form them, but not to prove them. Practical reason leads us to argue that moral law demands justice: happiness is proportional to virtue. Only providence (God) can guarantee this, it is not guaranteed in this life. Therefore unless God, freedom and immortality exist there is no such thing as virtue.

*Kant on morals*

Kant wished to establish a totally independent theory of morals, relying neither upon theology nor physics.

All moral concepts originate *a priori* in human reason. Moral worth only comes into being when one acts in accordance with one's sense of duty. It is not enough to be virtuous out of self-interest or to act kindly because one is naturally disposed to be kind. All nature acts according to laws. The very core of morality is the power of acting according to moral law. That is an objective law that compels the will. Kant calls this an *imperative*. The *hypothetical imperative* says: 'You must do *x* if you wish to achieve *y*.' The *categorical imperative* says: 'You must do *x*, what you want to achieve does not come into it, it is your duty, it is an obligation.'

There is only one *categorical imperative*: 'Act only according to a principle if at the same time you are certain you would like that principle to become a universal law.' Kant held the *categorical imperative* to be synthetic *a priori*. He deduced its content from the concept of law.

Appraisal

Kant's notion of synthetic *a priori* propositions is still debated. Many maintain that the rules of logic, the laws of geometry and arithmetic are all synthetic *a priori*. Many more dispute this, saying that all *a priori* propositions are analytic, an exercise in refined definition, merely making more explicit knowledge that is already contained in the meaning of any term. It has been objected that pure geometry may well be *a priori*, but it is not synthetic. Empirical geometry (a part of physics) is synthetic, not *a priori*.

Try to compile a short list of (say five) *a priori* propositions. How did you come by these *a priori* propositions? Try the same with a short list of synthetic propositions. How did you come by these synthetic propositions? What might be a synthetic *a priori* proposition?

Kant's treatment of the categories and the application of notions of space and time to them resulted in what he called *antinomies* (contradictions). This discussion of antinomies greatly influenced Hegel who used antinomies in his dialectic.

Kant held that the purely intellectual use of reason led to fallacies; reason is only rightly used when it is directed towards moral ends.

Kant's moral theory is held by many to be incomplete. It is based solely on the notion of obligation or law. There is no discussion of the moral content of an action, the context of a moral action, the intention of an action, the consequences of an action, the consequences in a given context.

How compelling do you find the categorical imperative?

Some people have criticized Kant's theory of space and time as being too subjective. What, they ask, causes me to arrange the things I see, hear, feel, and so on in the way I do? Kant says the mind orders the raw material of sensation. But do I not order it this way because that is the way it is?

Furthermore, Einstein's theories seem to suggest that time may slow down or speed up. They further suggest that the mass of a body increases with its velocity. Thus time and space may not be absolute. How might this affect Kant's notion that space and time are essential categories of the mind?

# 10 Karl Marx: the March of History

Probably more than any other person alive, Karl Marx affected the history of the twentieth century. Countless workers toiled to realize the vision he expressed; revolutionary groups crawled through jungles to spread his ideas; students stood on barricades to bring about the order he had written of; world statesmen slept uneasily in their beds at the thought of him. Yet he himself, as far as we know, never handled a gun, stood on a barricade, or belonged to a revolutionary army; he spent most of his days in the reading room of the British Library. 'Workers of the World unite, you have nothing to lose but your chains' may have been his motto, but he himself went home to his family every evening, without ever bringing home a decent wage at the end of the week. He is buried in Highgate Cemetery in London. At one stage there were so many statues of Marx dotted around Russia that anyone would have thought him to be a native son, yet it was a country he never visited.

We shall take a quick look at Marx's life and at the ideas that shaped Marxist thought and where they came from. Many critics would not consider Marx to be a philosopher at all. This is because they consider philosophy to be mainly concerned with theory of knowledge: how we know we know. Nevertheless Marx's ideas do fit in with another way of looking at philosophy: the ongoing process of thought which is characterized by openness to the possibility of thinking otherwise. Marx certainly 'thought otherwise' and wanted others to think otherwise also. But his influence was mainly felt in economics and politics. However, when dealing with philosophers, it is the ideas that are important.

Karl Marx

## Life

Karl Marx was born in 1818, in Trier, which is in the western part of what is now the German Federal Republic, near its border with Luxembourg. (You can still see the house in which he was born.) Some of his forebears had been rabbis, but his parents had become Christian. Marx entered the University of Bonn at the age of 17, but following trouble there transferred to the University of Berlin. In 1843 he married. His wife came from an aristocratic background, and he remained devoted to her throughout his life. The couple left Germany for Paris, where Marx met Friedrich Engels. However, following revolutionary political activity, he and his family sought refuge in England, where they remained for the rest of their lives.

While in London, Marx continued his collaboration with Engels and together they published the *Communist Manifesto*. He studied and wrote tirelessly, but was continually plagued by poverty and illness, and much saddened by the deaths of three of his children. He longed fervently for social revolution, but in his thinking and polemical work was determined to be scientific rather than romantic. He always wanted to appeal to evidence. For Marx, matter, not spirit, was the driving force. Only the first part of his major work, *Capital* (*Das Kapital*), was published in his lifetime.

---

**Timeline**

1818  Birth of Karl Marx

1830  July revolution in France

      Independence of Belgium, Greece, Colombia, Venezuela, Ecuador

      France seizes Algeria

1841  Marx graduates from the University of Berlin

1842  Marx takes up journalism

1843  Marx marries and goes to Paris

1847  Marx arrives in London; collaborates with Engels

1848  Marx and Engels publish the *Communist Manifesto*

      Proclamation of the Second Republic in France

      Insurrections in Italy, Austria, Hungary and a number of German states

1859  Darwin's *Origin of Species*

1864  First Workers' International in London

1865  Abolition of slavery in the USA

1867  Publication of *Capital*, Book I

1883  Death of Karl Marx

---

## Thought

Any discussion of Marxism inevitably involves technical jargon. So before we get involved with the ideas themselves, it might be a good idea to run through a number of influences on Marx and some of the technical terms he used.

*Influences*

There were three main influences on Marx: German philosophy, French social theory and British economic theory.

Friedrich Hegel was born in Stuttgart in 1770 and died in Berlin in 1831. He taught philosophy at Iena, Heidelberg and Berlin. Logic, philosophy of nature and philosophy of Spirit are the three elements in his theory of dialectical development. This is a form of thought which proceeds by overcoming contradictions.

Ludwig Feuerbach was born in Landshut in 1804 and died near Nuremberg in 1872. He rejected the idealism of Hegel and developed a philosophy of physical matter. He strongly criticized notions of God and of religion.

Pierre Joseph Proudhon was born in Besançon in 1809 and died in Paris in 1865. He is considered to be the founder of anarchism. He taught that only the disappearance of capitalist profit and the provision of free credit would be capable of eliminating social injustices. His refusal to put up with the authoritarian solutions of communism earned him the hostility of Marx.

Adam Smith was born in Kirkcaldy in Scotland in 1723 and died in Edinburgh in 1790. He believed in *laissez-faire* economics, thinking that human beings best contribute to the general interest by searching out their personal interest. In particular he distinguished between use-value and exchange-value.

---

**Determinism** is the philosophical doctrine that all decisions, acts, events are the inevitable consequence of past history. Such previous circumstances are environmental, physical or psychological conditions and do not depend upon human will.

*Laissez-faire* is the economic doctrine that government should not interfere with commerce.

**Use-value** is the value of something to you because you need to use it.

**Exchange-value** is how something is valuable to you because you can trade it for something else.

> **The law of diminishing returns** is the theory that after a certain point, profits decrease in proportion to the amount of further investment made.
>
> The **theory of surplus value** is the difference between the value of a product that labour has produced and the price of labour as paid out in wages.

David Ricardo was born in London in 1772 and died in Gloucestershire in 1823. An economist, he is responsible for elaborating the law of diminishing returns and the theory of surplus value.

## Dialectical materialism

The dialectic was a logical process originally attributed to Hegel.

- A *thesis* (an idea, an argument) is stated.
- This causes one to think of its opposite: the *antithesis.*
- There is a clash between thesis and *antithesis.*

This conflict is resolved into a *synthesis* which brings together both thesis and antithesis. This synthesis proposes a higher order than found in either thesis or antithesis.

This synthesis becomes in turn thesis, and the process starts all over again. For Hegel, it is a process involving spirit, but Marx held that matter is the only reality, so his application of the idea is called dialectical materialism.

## Marx's theory of history

The course of economic and political history so far has been:

- There were kings/rulers with absolute power. This is the thesis.
- At the other end of the scale were the dispossessed/slaves. This is the antithesis.

- These two cooperated and formed a civil society in which each contributed to the other. It was called feudalism. This is its synthesis.

- This synthesis in turn broke down into lords (the new thesis) and serfs (the new antithesis).
- The two cooperated together and formed a capitalistic society (a further synthesis).
- Capitalistic society broke down in turn into employers/capital (a fresh thesis), with employees/labour (as antithesis).
- The new synthesis was Marxist communism.

Marx held that matter is the only reality and applied the dialectic to economic conditions. He regarded mechanical explanations as fitting for physics and chemistry. Their methods therefore should not be adopted by the social sciences where matters of historical development come into play. The dialectic was for Marx a logical method, dealing with a developing subject matter and showing the inevitability of its development. The dialectic is a theory of progress. It explains and it also evaluates.

Hegel and Marx believed that the dialectic was a necessary law of nature. It laid down the course of history. It is the dialectic that controls the world. Human beings cannot alter the course of history. The highest moral value is to support and smooth the progress of the inevitable course of history.

Marxists claim that each new synthesis is ethically superior to the one that went before. Thus people, as they struggle to build a communist society, are engaging in a quasi-ethical struggle for what, by a law of historical determinism, must be better.

## Marx's notion of class

Everybody belongs to a social class. This is decided by the economic means and conditions of production. Each class will develop its own opposition (dialectic) and lead to strife. The rise of socialism will come about when strife leads to revolution, followed by the installation of a classless society where there is no further exploitation of the workers, for the means of production are now controlled by those same workers.

## Ideology

Marx held that each 'social class' has a group unity: rather like the nation. Each class acts together in history and produces typical ideas and beliefs. An individual's convictions, preferences and reasoning are a reflection of the ideas produced by that person's 'class'. Such ideas reflect characteristic core ideas for conduct: individuals are frequently unaware of this 'collective mindset'. Instead of expressing ideas which they have thought about and believe to be true, individuals unwittingly express the prejudices of their 'class'.

Such representative ideas are also misrepresentations. They are in fact quite different from what they seem: their compelling force arises out of the social position of each class and how it relates to economic production. Each of us has the sort of ideas that the members of our class usually have. We are convinced they are valid ideas because they appeal to our interests, the interests of our class. The forces of production are cunning in creating illusions in order to realize their own purpose. In this way each class gives birth to its own suitable ideology. 'Ideology' is a powerful weapon in controversy. It can be turned against all theory (including Marxist theory) in order to reveal it as 'special pleading'.

## Marx's attack on capitalism

Economic value for Marx is the cost that goes into producing something so that others will want to exchange something else for it. What makes something costly is the amount of labour that goes into producing it.

Ordinary workers have no capital and are therefore forced to sell their labour. But the items produced in this way have greater value than the wages the labourers receive for producing them. The difference between the economic value of the product and the wages received by the labourers who produced it is called *surplus value*. The employer takes the surplus value and uses it in many ways, most frequently as profit. This surplus value marks the conflict between capital and labour, employer and employee.

## Alienation

Marx used the term *alienation* to describe the feelings of purposelessness that human beings have in a depersonalized society. In a modern technological society most people do not carry out or achieve a complete process. They only carry out parts of a process. For example, a worker in a car factory spends all day putting on door handles and does nothing else. There is no sense that workers in a factory can claim to have made a car. They can have no sense of achievement from realizing a finished product. They feel a separation from all accomplishment, from all productive processes; they have lost control over them. This feeling of separation and loss is called *alienation*.

To get more profit entrepreneurs must compete with other entrepreneurs and undercut them. They will then sell more and get more profit. The only way they can realistically do this is by using inexpensive labour. To gain more and more profit employers must, according to Marx, pay their employees less and less. Thus capitalists get richer and labourers get poorer.

Capital imposes immoral conditions on how human beings relate to each other. So capitalism, as a fundamentally immoral system, must be replaced by a system where control of the means of production rests not with capital but with labour.

Marx held that in the modern industrial world human beings are cut off from each other and become insecure. This state is of our own making. We have created a technical world but cannot control it. We alienate ourselves from what we value most. Marx called this *self-alienation*.

Human beings in a capitalist society also practise fetishism: they value what they produce more than they value other human beings.

The greatest wound that capitalism has inflicted on human beings is to expect them to function like machines; the only value is market value: human values are systematically disallowed.

## Marxist revolution

Marx's philosophy of history is concerned with a particular grouping of economic forces and interests: feudalism (interests of landowners), capitalism (interests of employers) and socialism (interests of wage-earners). Marx considered class to be the means by which the dialectical movement progressed. He could not, on the basis of materialism alone, claim that socialism was ethically superior; it was, however, favoured by the dialectical movement and was thus inevitable. In so far as the dialectical movement was progress this gave socialism a form of superior moral value. Marx's examination of the conditions of the workers under the capitalism of his day was incisive and by and large accurate. His writings combined penetrating analysis with calm reflection and clarion calls to revolution.

---

**Materialism** is the philosophical doctrine that physical matter, including its movements and adaptation, is the only reality and that everything in the universe can be explained in terms of physical laws. This includes mind, thought, will and feeling.

**Empiricism** is the philosophical doctrine that the experiences of the senses (touch, sight, hearing, taste, smell) are the only source of knowledge.

---

Marx held that his use of materialism was scientific: he believed that social studies could be precise and certain. Materialism deals with what is matter of fact and empirical. He backed up his theories and policies with an impressive volume of historical and economic research. Materialism, for Marx, implied aggressive atheism and the rejection of religion, which he viewed as a conservative force. As the 'opium of the people' it supplied fantasy consolations, hindered rational effort and dissuaded the oppressed from making efforts to better their lot. He was blind to its potential as an *energizer*: the value that deeply held conviction (rather than rational reflection) possesses for promoting action and change.

Materialism and the dialectic, in Marx's view, implied revolution: the existing system is overthrown. This is in contrast with reform, where the existing system is improved. In the French Revolution a 'political revolution' had occurred. Here the middle classes (the bourgeoisie), the owners of the means of economic production, had seized political control from the nobility (feudalism). Dialectical materialism implied that a new 'social revolution', which will uproot the sources of exploitation and social inequality, must inevitably take place. This will happen when control of the system of production is transferred to the proletariat (those exploited by the bourgeoisie). Marx strongly rejected the notion that the laws of a capitalist economy are unchangeable and eternal.

---

### *Capital* (1867)

Marx's socialism arose from a critique of Hegel. Marx's theory is one of development: each economic stage is marked by a typical way of producing and exchanging goods. Changes in production and distribution are the primary factors in the dialectic of history. The whole process is 'dialectical': working out the internal tensions which arise from the disparities between an evolving system of production and the ideology of an older persisting system.

- Material or economic forces are primary. The evolution of the human race arises from our bodily necessities.
- The political condition of a society at any period reflects the requirements of the class which dominates production and is expressed in its ideology.
- The dominating class arouses resentment and this results in a 'class-war'.

- The production forces must develop before the dialectical transformation can take place.
- The system is intensely deterministic.
- When the 'dictatorship of the proletariat' is finally established this will lead to the end of the long series of social struggles.
- The state is an instrument of oppression which is necessary only as long as the class war continues. When all classes are abolished the state also will pass away.
- The 'dictatorship of the proletariat' will achieve the socialization of the means of production. This process is to be managed by an elite group of revolutionary Marxists.

## Appraisal

Marx's work was one of the most important bodies of thought to influence the twentieth century. It is important to realize that his socialism did not arise from sympathy with the oppressed, but from a critique of Hegel.

Some aspects of Marx's work have been discredited. This is due partly to later historical events and partly to critical thought. Marx was less of a philosopher (one who critiqued existing modes and proposed new modes of knowing and believing) than a promoter and energizer of political activism. His work contained a great deal of historical analysis, but essentially it looked to the future and sought to foretell what, by the laws of historical development, must take place. We stand in a position of hindsight. Marx did not have the benefit of this hindsight. This allows us a privileged view of the weaknesses of his theory.

Marx underestimated the power of capitalism to fit itself to changing circumstances. He believed that capitalism depended on a progressive reduction of workers' living standards. In fact capitalism has proved itself capable of raising salaries and improving working conditions, health, welfare and educational provision. Nevertheless in Marx's time many of the criticisms he levelled against it were accurate and pertinent. Many would say that capitalism's recent development was partly due to the justified criticisms, backed by the real fear of social revolution, which Marx levelled against it.

The experience of living under Marxist regimes has not led people to renounce personal convictions, goals, freedom or ethical beliefs. They are frequently held and nurtured against the 'determinism' of dialectical materialism. Part of the shock of the collapse of communism in Europe has been how age-old tensions, be they ethnic, religious or historical have resurfaced when everybody thought they had been wiped away by the struggle to build socialist societies.

Marx's critique of religion as the 'opium of the people' ignored the capacity of conviction to energize. Indeed, the excesses of many communist regimes themselves contributes to the body of evidence that non-rational belief in fantastic panaceas promotes rather than deadens extreme action, and that Marxism was itself incapable of applying an ethical critique or regulation of such programmes. However, it must be pointed out that communist regimes have always been adaptations rather than pure applications of Marx's thought.

On a more theoretical level, we may note that though Marx condemned many non-revolutionary schemes of socialism as palliatives and utopian, his own idea of a classless society where government would wither away because there was no need for it had similarly unrealistic, utopian tendencies. Moreover, his notion of ideology, which is actually quite vague, can be levelled against Marxist thought itself which (it could be argued) is also a form of special pleading.

Marx's version of the class-war was an oversimplification of the facts. He recognized only two classes. He believed that salaried employees and professionals (middle-class wage-earners) would be absorbed into the proletariat. This did not happen. In fact the tendency has been for assimilation to be in the other direction, though the term 'middle classes' now means something subtly different from what it did in Marx's day.

Do you see any value at all in Marx's critique of capitalism? How did you come to these judgements? What would be your approach towards a resolution of the problems? How did Marx go about suggesting an alternative? How does your methodology differ from that of Marx?

Marx's chief value now lies in the stress he laid on the economic interpretation of history. Amongst his intellectual offspring are those modern historians who seek to understand historical events by analysing the economic factors governing them. Politicians now usually see their chief task as promoting general social and economic development; in this they are more indebted to Marx than they often realize.

Finally, Marx's notion of predetermined stages of history, the inevitable working out of dialectical materialism, has more to do with optimism, quasi-religious faith or fatalism than with scientific thought.

# 11  Friedrich Nietzsche: the Will to Power

Would you ever think of praising difficulty and wretchedness as the prizes of a life well lived? Do you prefer to think of the goals of life as rational thought, calm, detachment, ability to think through problems and arrive at reasonable solutions? Do you think that philosophy books should be the measured description of developing thought? Think again! Nietzsche's writing can be outspoken and rough. He has no difficulty in calling those who disagree with him 'blockheads'. He is about to turn your ideas upside-down, but don't let him blow your mind! Respond with a measured, detached and critical evaluation.

Friedrich Nietzsche

## Life

Friedrich Wilhelm Nietzsche was born in Saxony (in what is now east Germany) in 1844. His father was a Lutheran minister who died when Friedrich was 5. He was brought up by his mother, grandmother and several aunts. The home atmosphere was devout.

The young Nietzsche attended the local gymnasium or secondary school from 1854 to 1858, and later went to boarding school. He developed an early admiration for the genius of Greece; he was also fond of music and poetry.

In 1864 Nietzsche entered the University of Bonn and read philology, later moving to the University of Leipzig. By this time he no longer considered himself a Christian, being an admirer of Schopenhauer and attracted by his atheism. Nietzsche was appointed professor of philosophy at the University of Basel without having completed his doctorate. He gave his first lecture there in 1869. The following year saw the outbreak of the Franco-Prussian War, during which Nietzsche served in the ambulance corps. He was for a while seriously ill, but later resumed work at Basel. During this period he formed a close friendship with the composer Richard Wagner and visited him frequently at his home on Lake Lucerne.

Early writings such as *Thoughts out of Season* were controversial and brought no academic credit. Nietzsche began to drift away from Wagner, considering some of his work to be 'too Christian'. His philosophical thought was never particularly coherent: early writings tend to attack the rational spirit of Socrates, whereas those of a later period tend to praise his rational outlook and also that of the French Enlightenment. However, the thought of major thinkers does evolve. Nietzsche started to attack metaphysics and seek a materialistic basis for morals. Good and evil were originally just ways of pointing out that certain actions benefited society; others were bad for it. Once people had forgotten this entirely instrumental basis for ethical judgement they started to think that good and evil were absolute terms.

Bad health and disgust with things in general led him to resign his chair in 1879. From then on he led a somewhat nomadic life, seeking a healthy place to live – he was particularly fond of mountains. His 1882 work *Joyful Wisdom* attacked Christianity as 'hostile to life'. Later on he developed the idea that there are cycles in time recurring over and over again: all that has been is inevitably repeated. This came to him with the force of a special revelation – his message to the planet – and it is written as if spoken by the Persian wise man Zarathustra in *Thus Spoke Zarathustra* (*Also sprach, Zarathustra*). This is probably his best-known book, containing his ideas of eternal recurrence, Superman and the transvaluation of values. This represents yet another stage in Nietzsche's thought. It is a visionary book, presented in declamatory and prophetic tones. *Beyond Good and Evil*, published in 1886, is a more measured outline of Nietzsche's thinking.

## Timeline

1844  Birth of Friedrich Wilhelm Nietzsche

1848  Revolutions in Europe

1849  Death of Nietzsche's father

1854  Nietzsche enters local gymnasium

1859  Darwin's *Origin of Species*

1864  Nietzsche attends University of Bonn, later moves to Leipzig

1869  Nietzsche appointed professor of philosophy at University of
        Basel; friendship with Wagner

1870  Nietzsche serves in Franco-Prussian War

1871  Bismarck becomes Chancellor of unified Germany

1873–79  Nietzsche's *Thoughts out of Season*

1876  End of Nietzsche's friendship with Wagner
        Inauguration of Bayreuth theatre with Wagner's *The Ring*

1882  Nietzsche's *Joyful Wisdom* published

1883–85  *Thus Spoke Zarathustra*

1886  *Beyond Good and Evil*

1888  William II becomes German Kaiser

1889  Nietzsche's illness and eventual insanity

1900  Death of Nietzsche

Later Nietzsche published ferocious attacks on his former friend Wagner, and subsequent writings began to reflect his mental instability. He was admitted to a clinic in Basel in 1889; on discharge he lived with his sister at Weimar. He was now famous, but considered insane. This was probably the result of an early attack of syphilis that remained untreated. He died in 1900. He never married.

## Thought

Nietzsche's outlook has been called 'aristocratic anarchism'. He promotes two sets of values: on the one hand, war, ruthlessness, pride in what one is; on the other, philosophy, music, poetry. He was a professor of philosophy in energetic opposition to the dominant political, ethical and social stances of his day.

Nietzsche's motives were ethical. He considered certain great qualities to be desirable but only achievable by the few. It is the business of the many to promote and make possible the excellence of the few. They should not have any claim to happiness or well-being. True virtue is not profitable or prudent: it isolates those who practise it from others; it is against order and it harms inferiors. Superior beings should make war on their inferiors; the democratic tendencies of the age are the promotion of mediocrity.

Nevertheless Nietzsche did not promote his views so that the superior could live lives of pampered indulgence. He believed in Spartan discipline and thought that one must be able to endure as well as to inflict pain. Strength of will is the supreme virtue. Compassion is weakness. He was a believer in the hero rather than the state.

Nietzsche was contemptuous of women, an outlook that was backed up neither by reason nor experience. He was hostile to Christianity, alleging that it promoted a 'slave mentality'. He had no interest in the truth or untruth of Christianity; he was antagonistic simply because it denies the basic difference of value between one individual and another. The New Testament is the idealization of 'a totally ignoble species of man'. It aims at taming the heart of man;

it tries to destroy the strong, to break their spirit and undo their will to power – and this is all wrong.

Nietzsche's noble man will be cruel, will sacrifice his fellow humans, will be disciplined and will practise violence and cunning in war.

---

### Thus Spoke Zarathustra (1885)

- Life is the will to power, and whoever wishes to live truly must overcome the beliefs and conventions of ordinary mortals: become a 'Superman'.
- The Christian virtues of pity and meekness seek to corrupt people, to destroy their willpower, in order to make them submit to those who live conventionally.
- Those who do not have the courage to live, seek to escape by sleeping, prizing the soul over the body, seeking peace instead of war.
- Superman is virtuous by freeing himself from belief in God, and from the illusion of an afterlife. Superman cannot abide ordinary people. He is happy, surpassing those who live by false hopes and beliefs.
- Worship is a return to childhood.

---

### Nietzsche's masks

Nietzsche's thought underwent 'stages'. In an early stage it was rationalistic and critical. (He later described this as an 'eccentric pose' which had to be discarded so that he could break through to his true nature.) Nietzsche himself thought of these stages as masks, which he had to discard so that his thought might advance and his true self emerge. The mask was what everybody saw, beneath it his true thought developed and at the right time was revealed.

At a later stage Nietzsche was testing himself: checking to see if he had the strength to say yes to life, enduring every moment of his life, sufferings and humiliations. This led to his notion of Superman: a myth that allowed those who were a higher type of person to develop their potentialities. 'The criterion of truth is the intensification of the feeling of power.' Thought is an instrument which helps an individual to achieve his possibilities.

### The will to power

The will to power is the source of what is and what ought to be. The weaker people, members of the herd, are unable to affirm life, they construct a morality that will allow them to continue to escape from it; moreover, their morality allows them to gain power. They exalt their own weakness when they promote pity, solidarity, etc. They are incapable of practising 'voluptuousness, power of passion and selfishness'; only the strong can do that and they stand to suffer at the hands of those who dare to be ruthless, so they seek to tie down the noble and healthy with prohibitions.

If the weak cannot drag themselves up to the level of those above them, they can at least drag those above down to their own level. They practise resentment: the resentment of the ordinary for the extraordinary. They wish to destroy and abase those whose abilities show up their own weakness. When communism threatens, fascism galvanizes against it the resentment of the lower middle classes. The strong soul does not know resentment. He openly and frankly admits his will to power; he glories in it.

---

**Materialism** is the doctrine that nothing exists except matter and that all thought, feeling, mind or will may be explained in terms of that physical reality.

**Instrumental** means considering something only from the point of view of how it can be used to achieve something else, never from the point of view of its own value or merit.

**Absolute** means existing independently of any condition, limit or representation; being entire and of itself; having its own authority.

---

---

### *Beyond Good and Evil* (1886)

- Ideas which preserve life and add to an individual's power are more important than ideas approved by logicians and seekers after the absolute.
- Metaphysical interest in the freedom of the will should be discarded in favour of the strength of the will.
- Man must turn conventional values upside down in order to live creatively. Values of society were invented by the weak to allow them to overcome the strong.
- Scientific minds are weak when they do not pass judgement. Whenever one denies the will one denies life.
- Progress in life is only possible when there are men of action prepared to trust will and instinct. When the will to power asserts itself, new values, going beyond conventional values, come into being.

---

### *The transvaluation of all values*

The will to power leads to the 'transvaluation of values': current moral judgement is abolished, purified and a new set of values proposed. What has been forbidden for centuries, by the machinations of the weak, is now to be promoted and gloried in. But it is a call to discipline, suffering and achievement. Even if each of us begins with a rule imposed: 'Thou shalt'; each of us must confront it with 'I will'.

Nietzsche's hero is the man who raises himself above his fellows by his own powers; he refuses to apologize for his superiority, but boldly lives it out. The health-giving qualities are being hard, pitiless and stern. (This aspect of his thought was much prized by fascist organizations of the 1930s.)

### *Superman*

*Superman is the meaning of the earth.*
*Man is a rope stretched between beast and Superman.*

In general, nineteenth-century thinkers saw Darwin's theory of evolution as a diminishing of the human; Nietzsche, on the other hand, dared to proclaim the positive possibilities of this development.

Nietzsche never implied that existing groups of men were biologically superior to others, nor did he promote Aryan superiority. (He was in fact contemptuous of the German people.) What he meant was that Superman is the being who will come when man learns to transcend himself. Superman will be a figure of vitality, power, exuberance and self-expression and will be capable of combining all those qualities in a harmonious way. He will be an individual who is confident, alert, disciplined and strong. He will be far superior to the herd, which will only be able to admire him.

In this representation of Nietzsche's thought the language is deliberately sexist. This is the language Nietzsche would have used and meant.

### Nietzsche's influence

Nietzsche had great influence, but rarely upon philosophers. His influence was rather amongst those with artistic and literary interests. He prophesied an era of great wars, but did not live to see either world war. He is accused of having an influence over fascist thinkers with their promotion of 'male' culture, their backing for the superior race and their disciplined militarism invading all aspects of civil society.

---

**Fascism**

Many hold that Nietzsche was one of the inspirations for fascism, but in fact fascism would probably have arisen without him. Nevertheless it is interesting to note briefly important points of fascist doctrine:

- Fascism was a revolt against reason: will and act were self-justifying.
- Obedience was to a higher law: an objective will.
- Duty, authority and discipline replaced happiness and freedom.

- The state was all-important and directed the economic system.
- All economic classes were to be reconciled in the interest of the unity of the state.
- It appealed to emotion to release the people's energies.
- Parliament and the judiciary were not independent: their functions were subsumed by the executive branch of government.
- The ideal form of organization was military discipline.
- The nation was credited with the gift of instinct which allowed it to select a leader and follow him.
- The central political principle was 'the leader' and beneath him an 'ascending series of personalities'.
- The 'purity of the race' was promoted.

There are many elements in this list with which Nietzsche would have disagreed. He was not, for example, a lover of the German peoples, his notion of discipline and ruthlessness had to do with the promotion of the individual, rather than the group. On the other hand, fascists themselves saw echoes of treasured attitudes in his thought: Superman for instance, but on their terms rather than Nietzsche's.

## Appraisal

Nietzsche's thought is the means by which he, as an individual, tried to realize what he was capable of. It was not philosophy in the sense of critique of knowledge, but rather 'philosophy' in the sense of inspiration, vision and impulse.

Nietzsche's passion was to 'think differently'. He had no time for ready-made solutions or systems; he energetically forged a new way of thinking and urged a break with ways of thought which previously had held sway.

His 'aristocratic' values were a rudimentary ethic rather than a political theory. He did not propose a theory of government. He admired a type of man who might be called 'aristocratic'. But this was an aristocracy of ability, will and action rather than an aristocracy of breeding. This aristocracy has more willpower, courage, ruthlessness and inclination to impose power and less sympathy, gentleness and fear.

Whereas Marx is the philosopher for whom all individual desires and actions are to be submitted to the judgement of the group, the proletariat, Nietzsche is the philosopher for whom the considerations of the group are swept aside in order to promote the desires of the strong individual.

Most moralists promote sympathy, denounce suffering and wish to improve the universal lot. Nietzsche denounced sympathy, exalted suffering and delighted in those who exercise power over others.

In appraising the philosophy of Nietzsche we might say that there is no purely rational answer to him, just as his thought is not a purely rational construct. There is no objective set of values or objective knowledge of good and evil to which we can appeal. One can follow the precepts of a revered moral teacher such as Buddha, Jesus or Mohammed. Or else one can consult one's emotions: 'I don't like suffering, I wish people to be more sympathetic, I reject the exercise of power over others. Therefore I dislike Nietzsche!' But this is not a rational refutation of his ideas; it is a statement of personal preference.

Finally, we might ask the question: what are the positive values of Nietzsche's stance?

# 12  Ludwig Wittgenstein: Language and Reality

Wittgenstein is frequently portrayed as a 'difficult' philosopher. He was an original thinker, often presented as not only having produced one highly original philosophy, but two. He was chiefly interested in problems of logic and problems of language.

## Life

Ludwig Wittgenstein was born in 1889 in Vienna. His father was in the iron and steel industry and the family was extremely wealthy. Ludwig's grandfather was a Jew who had converted to Protestantism; his mother was a Catholic, which is how Ludwig himself was brought up. The family was very musical. Ludwig was given his early education privately at home. He showed considerable talent with his hands, building working machines out of scrap.

Wittgenstein did not go to school until he was 14. Adolf Hitler was a fellow pupil, but this fact is coincidental. Wittgenstein trained first of all as an engineer, in Berlin; later he did a postgraduate course in Manchester: in aeronautics, in particular the combustion of high-pressure gases. This led him to be curious about the foundations of mathematics, which in turn brought him to philosophy.

Wittgenstein started to write a book on the foundations of mathematics and logic. He showed it to the German philosopher and mathematician Gottlob Frege. Frege recommended that Wittgenstein go to Cambridge and study mathematics under Bertrand Russell. (Russell came from an aristocratic English background; he had written a seminal work on mathematics, *Principia Mathematica*. He was also a world-famous philosopher). The two formed an enduring friendship. The story goes that Russell and G.E. Moore, another famous Cambridge philosopher at Trinity College, were discussing new students and came to Wittgenstein. 'I cannot make up my mind', said one, 'whether he is an idiot or a genius.' 'Why?' asked the other. 'Because he always looks puzzled during my lectures.'

Russell was persuaded that Wittgenstein was a genius and showed him the text of a major work on theory of knowledge that he was writing. Wittgenstein criticized it so profoundly that, in disgust, Russell decided to leave the writing of a major work on logical theory to him. Wittgenstein often spent all night walking up and down the floor of Russell's rooms wrestling with the problems of logic and also with his sins. Russell was afraid to suggest it was time for bed in case he became suicidal. Eventually Wittgenstein left Cambridge, but without taking a BA. He went to Norway to meditate alone on logic.

War broke out in 1914, and Wittgenstein volunteered as a gunner in the Austrian army. He experienced all of the harsh conditions of war, but saw little action. He continued to make notes on logical theory and started to develop them into a book. This was later to become his major work *Tractatus Logico-Philosophicus*. It is said that he carried it around in his knapsack for the duration of the war.

His experience as a soldier, his bravery, his insistence on being sent to where there was most danger, won Wittgenstein several medals, but also profoundly influenced the direction of his thought so that it became a reflection on both logic and ethics. Cambridge University Press refused to publish his *Tractatus* and indeed it published none of his other work. Instead, his writings were published in Oxford. The philosophizing he practised, with a heavy concentration on linguistic analysis, was often referred to as Oxford philosophy, despite the fact that it had been developed at Cambridge.

The chief thrust of Wittgenstein's philosophy at this time was to express what can be said as clearly as possible. This draws a boundary around what can be thought. About all else we must be silent: but this is what really matters.

After the First World War Wittgenstein returned to Austria. His father had died in 1913 and Ludwig was now extremely rich, but he gave most of his money away, usually to artists in need of help. He decided he had solved all the problems of philosophy; there was nothing more for him to do, so he would be a schoolteacher. He taught in a number of village primary schools. But he insisted on teaching complicated mathematics to his young charges, both boys and girls, which was unusual for those times. The educational authorities felt he was a gifted teacher; he taught by getting his pupils to question and to build models and machines. Unfortunately he often got impatient and was accused of beating them when they did not understand. The locals found him authoritarian, aristocratic and dislikeable. It is true that he was very difficult to get along with – in any society. His failure as a schoolteacher affected him profoundly and to recover he withdrew for a time to a monastery.

Wittgenstein gave up schoolteaching, returned to Vienna and became interested in modern, functional house-designing. He built a house for his sister. An austere building, it was designed to be totally appropriate to its use. It still stands in Vienna. Whilst in Vienna, Wittgenstein met a Swiss friend of his sister's called Marguerite, with whom he fell in love. He wanted to marry her, and took her away to spend time in his house in Norway. However, whilst there he spent much of the night in prayer, and she, presumably feeling somewhat neglected, decided to cut her losses and left after two weeks. They remained friends, but Wittgenstein never married.

By this time, Wittgenstein had some contact with members of the Vienna Circle, a group of thinkers interested in making philosophy scientific. In 1929 Wittgenstein returned to Cambridge and presented the *Tractatus* as his thesis. Moore and Russell were his examiners. It is said that at the oral during which he was to defend his thesis he ended up clapping them both on the shoulders and telling them not to worry, they would never understand his work! It is also said that Moore's report to the examinations board read: 'In my opinion Mr Wittgenstein's thesis is a work of genius; be that as it may, it is well up to the standard required for the award of a Doctorate of philosophy of the University of Cambridge.'

Wittgenstein now embarked on a period of teaching philosophy at Cambridge. He himself lived most frugally. The only furniture in his rooms was a table, a few deckchairs and a campbed!

Wittgenstein gave no formal lectures. He simply stood in his rooms and thought out loud. He had no notes. There were long periods of silence. He often cursed his own stupidity and also clashed with his listeners. His students had the impression they were in the presence of deep seriousness and originality of thought. How anybody thought they were being adequately prepared for a degree is impossible to guess, and it is unlikely that his behaviour and methods would have suited everybody. However, he did put together two series of notes which he gave to his students so that they might 'take away something in their hands if not in their heads'. These are published under the title *The Blue and Brown Books*, because they were originally handed out with blue and brown covers.

Wittgenstein refused to teach philosophy during the Second World War, but worked instead as a porter in a London hospital. He fell in love with two young men, one during, one after the war. They were both Cambridge students. The first relationship brought Ludwig much suffering, but the second much joy.

In 1947 Wittgenstein resigned his fellowship and went to live in an isolated house on the west coast of Ireland. It was here he wrote his most important work, *Philosophical Investigations*.

Soon after this, he became ill. He was diagnosed with prostate cancer and died in Cambridge in 1951. He continued to work on philosophical problems until he lost consciousness on the day before he died.

## Thought

### The importance of logic

Logic was most important for Aristotle and also for the scholastic philosophers of the Middle Ages; this was the 'tool' they would use to produce clear ideas, valid arguments and sure conclusions. By the late nineteenth century logic had been neglected for many years. Indeed, it was frequently assumed that all the problems of logic had been solved. However, during the late nineteenth and

## Timeline

1889  Birth of Ludwig Wittgenstein in Vienna

1903  Wittgenstein goes to school at Linz

1906  Studies engineering at Berlin

1908  Goes to Manchester as a research student

1911  To Trinity College, Cambridge, where he meets Russell

1913  Death of Wittgenstein's father; Wittgenstein goes to Norway to
         be alone

1914–18  First World War; Wittgenstein volunteers as a private soldier
             and is made a prisoner of war

1917  Russian Revolution

1918  Wittgenstein becomes a rural schoolteacher

1921  Publication of the *Tractatus Logico-Philosophicus*

1926  Wittgenstein gives up teaching

1929  Returns to Cambridge
         Wall Street crash

1939–45  Second World War; Wittgenstein working in London as
             hospital porter

1947  Wittgenstein goes to live on the west coast of Ireland

1951  Wittgenstein dies in Cambridge

1958  Publication of *The Blue and Brown Books* and *Philosophical
         Investigations*

early twentieth centuries logic returned in force as a major philosophical problem. It has since been very important in colleges in
Britain and America.

It was Gottlob Frege who kick-started the revolution in logic. Frege
saw that mathematics and language had much in common. Numbers,
he said, are not things in themselves but concepts which describe
things. Concepts are not objects in themselves but are used to describe
objects. Concepts in language can be put together to make sentences,
so concepts in mathematics (and logic) can be put together to make
sentences (now called propositions).

Frege talked about reference and sense. Reference has to do with what the sentence is about: the cat, the act of sitting and the mat in the sentence 'The cat sat on the mat.' Sense has to do with how they relate to each other.

Frege taught that we can understand what language and maths do without worrying about the content of the propositions. What is important is how the elements hold together, not what they refer to. So Frege developed a whole set of symbols to describe the way in which the elements of a proposition hold together.

The idea is that 'The cat sat on the mat' and 'The dog sat on the table' have the same structure. However, what do you say to 'The committee sat on the report'? Maybe Wittgenstein can help, eventually. But back to Frege.

It is the structure, the way the elements relate together, that we worry about when we ask if an argument is 'logical' or not. We don't have to worry about the sense of each individual proposition. This is called *symbolic logic*. It allows us to analyse the propositions of an argument in a way that is more accurate than Aristotle's.

*Wittgenstein's first philosophy*

Wittgenstein tried to show that logic and reality have the same structure. He presented his arguments in the *Tractatus Logico-Philosophicus*. It is a tightly controlled work expounding a highly restricted view of language. It sets out to draw limits around what can be clearly said and expressed. Wittgenstein criticized all views of language not based on logic. He also criticized attempts to say anything about subjects whose existence cannot be proved: art, religion, metaphysics and ethics. They all exist, but do the values they talk about have a sure, independent and incontrovertible foundation?

A statement can only have meaning if that statement refers in an obvious way to things actually in the world. He talked of 'logical atoms' which are facts that do not depend on other facts for their meaning. 'Logical atoms' cannot be divided into smaller independent facts. Here Wittgenstein's thought concentrates on what Frege called 'reference'.

The *Tractatus* consists of remarks, mainly about language, the world, logic and mathematics, but also finally about ethics and mysticism. It is structured as an organic unit, and arranged in seven main sections, with each section leading to dependent subsections, all tidily ordered and numbered. Each remark is supported and supports the ones around it. The opening words are

1     The world is all that is the case.

1.1    The world is the totality of facts not of things.

The last words are

6.54   My propositions serve as elucidations in the following way: anyone who understands me eventually recognizes them as nonsensical, when he has used them – as steps – to climb up beyond them. (He must, so to speak, throw away the ladder after he has climbed up it.)

        He must transcend these propositions, and then he will see the world aright.

7     What we cannot speak of we must pass over in silence.

---

**Logic** is the science of valid reasoning; the methodology used to achieve internal coherence in argument.

**Reference** is a theory of meaning holding that words refer to things in the world; we use the word 'hat' to refer to hats.

A **Proposition** is the meaning a sentence conveys. 'It was too dark for me to see' and 'I couldn't see because of the dark' are two different sentences, but they are just one proposition.

**Metaphysics** is the study of being as being; speculation about the meaning of what is; the study of first principles and first causes; the rational knowledge of those realities that go beyond us; the rational study of things in themselves.

**Ethics** is the study of the principles governing what is right and wrong. It is concerned with notions like 'Good', 'Obligation' and 'Duty'.

**Aesthetics** is the study of beauty and the responses we make to it.

> ### *Tractatus Logico-Philosophicus* (1921)
>
> - The world is made up of atomic facts; atomic facts are facts which cannot be analysed into more elemental facts.
> - Propositions are logical pictures of facts. A proposition and the fact it pictures have a common (logical) structure.
> - But a proposition only shows the form of a possible fact; it does not express it. When one can give the general form of propositions, one can give the essence of all description and of the world. We form propositions (1) by drawing from the class of elementary propositions and (2) by using different logical operations.
> - Philosophy is the process by which we clarify meaning. Propositions in natural science are meaningful. But it is impossible to say anything meaningful in ethics, aesthetics or metaphysics. Such attempts all involve the impossible task of talking about the world from the outside.

Wittgenstein saw the world as a totality of facts, not of things. Facts are logical entities; they can only be asserted or denied. They are not hard, red, round, etc. Things exist in space and time: they have shape colour, consistency, etc.

A fact could be otherwise: we have to be able to think that things could be otherwise independently of whether those different conditions are realized or not. Pictures of facts as we express them in language give us meaning. Wittgenstein saw the world consisting of simple objects fitting together like links in a chain and giving us states of affairs.

The purpose of philosophy is the logical clarification of our thoughts. Philosophy is an activity; it is not a body of teaching. We do philosophy when we make things clear. Logic shows logical form. It tells us nothing about what is in the world.

Whenever we make a stab at expressing absolute value we come up against the limits of language in various ways. Wittgenstein tried to express these as being:

(1) *at the level of existence*, where we are astonished at the very existence of the world;

(2) *at the level of our own subjectivity*, where we cannot feel totally safe no matter what happens;

(3) *at the level of ethics*, when we are guilty because we fail to measure up to an absolute requirement which in any case we could not express.

We cannot demonstrate the limits of language or of the world.

Wittgenstein held that every proposition, together with what it described, must have a logical form. But what is the logical form of a prayer, of an ethical precept, or of an insulting gesture? Because they communicate they must be forms of language. But are they permissible and is the straitjacket that Wittgenstein draped around what can and cannot be said tied too tightly?

## Wittgenstein's second philosophy

In this new philosophy, Wittgenstein's thought concentrated on what Frege called 'sense'. He decided that what a sentence meant (what language means) is not what the words refer to in the world outside, but the way in which words relate to each other. The way language works is not because it acts like an ideal logic, but because it follows its own working, which is the way people agree language works. This is not something that happens formally, but something the people in a language community grasp automatically.

If I say, 'The young rogue tried it on with the teacher and unbelievably he got away with it!' the meaning of the sentence has nothing to do with the logical structure of 'tried it on' or 'got away with it'. It has to do with the fact that a language community accepts that these combinations of words mean a certain thing and not something else. So Wittgenstein came to talk of *language games*.

We can perhaps now see a way to considering the meaning of 'The cat sat on the mat' and 'The committee sat on the report.' The sentences do *not* have the same logical structure. The language community aggress that 'sat on' means something different in each sentence. The difference does not have to be flagged. The language community is automatically aware of the games it plays and accepts them. Wittgenstein's second philosophy undermines his first.

We can never get outside language to the reality 'outside' language. We can only use language in order to talk about language. All language is shared by at least two people. There is no such thing as a 'private language'.

The *Philosophical Investigations* is a carefully crafted book. Its sentences are not so sharp and pointed as those in the *Tractatus*. The remarks are longer; there are also dialogues and a variety of positions are expressed. There are no logical symbols.

The *Philosophical Investigations* is about concepts of meaning, how we understand, about propositions and logic, mathematics, states of consciousness, and much more besides. Wittgenstein sought to express the connection between language and way of life. We are profoundly enmeshed in language confusion. But the language confusion we suffer from grew up because we have a tendency to think in that way.

---

### Philosophical Investigations (1958)

- Language is an activity which uses words as tools.
- Words are used in many ways. We understand them when we play the 'language games' that actually use words. Words are not labels for things.
- The meaning of a word is the way it is used in language.
- We understand talk about feelings because there is a 'grammar' of feelings. Those who know the language game can understand this grammar. Everything we have in our minds only makes sense in this way.
- Expecting, intending, remembering are ways of life made possible by language.
- Language itself is a way of life.

---

## Appraisal

The earlier philosophy had tried to unearth the essence of what is hidden from us. The new philosophy, seen by Wittgenstein as a form of therapy, did not try to explain – there is nothing hidden – it tries to set what is there before us.

Wittgenstein was teaching a skill, seeking to criticize, to free our minds from the bewitchment of our intelligence by means of language.

There is no such thing as pure thought. We do not put our thoughts into language. We cannot think unless we possess language.

Wittgenstein came to see 'truth' as a kind of language game. When we think about language we imagine we are standing outside language. There is language on the one hand, reality on the other. But look at a single book. How many objects do you see? One? But how many covers has the book? Does it have a detachable dust jacket? How many pages does it have? Are they all different objects? The answer is yes and no. It depends how you are determined to use language at that moment.

Wittgenstein was an influential contributor to what is now known as 'analytical philosophy' or 'linguistic philosophy'. Analytical philosophers frequently criticize 'continental philosophers' (philosophers who take their cue from forms of thinking prevalent in France and Germany and owing much to thinkers such as Hegel and Marx) for focusing on subjects about which it is hard to say anything with certainty. They are thinking of things like sociology, psychology, unconsciousness and political struggles. Analytical philosophers tend to eliminate these from their investigations. Continental philosophers reply that because these things are not certain it does not mean they are unimportant.

Can we have definite, unassailable knowledge in matters of ethics, religion, aesthetics and metaphysics? If so, how is it arrived at? If not, must all discussion of ethics, religion, aesthetics and metaphysics be abandoned? Do they have any value? What might their value be?

# 13 Martin Heidegger: We Have Forgotten Being

Martin Heidegger is one of the most foundational, enigmatic and personally controversial philosophers of the twentieth century. As the century progressed, it was evident that he had been an important influence on more and more thinkers, though mostly in continental Europe; as the century progressed, the account of his personal collusion with Nazi thought and practice has become more glaring; finally, at every point during that century, his writings were judged to be obscure to the point of unreadability.

Heidegger exercised a strong influence on Sartre, but also on a number of theologians, among them Karl Rahner and John Macquarrie (who, along with Edward Robinson, translated him into English). Others who have been profoundly influenced by his thought include Jacques Derrida, Michel Foucault, Hans Georg Gadamer and Jacques Lacan.

## Life

Martin Heidegger was born into a staunchly Catholic family in the Black Forest region of Baden in Germany on 26 September 1889. He studied philosophy at Freiburg, where Edmund Husserl was one of his teachers. Heidegger later taught at this same university, but also at the University of Marburg. He became Rector of the University of Freiburg in 1933.

On the occasion of Heidegger's installation as Rector he enthusiastically advocated the Nazi point of view, believing it would bring something new to Germany; he heralded it as a 'new dawn'. Ten months later he recognized his mistake, resigned his rectorship and withdrew from politics. He lived in increasing isolation in the Black Forest, adopting the simple life. He died in 1976, having been severely criticized over a period of 30 years because of his earlier stance.

Heidegger did partially address the issue of his early support for Nazism in an interview, but forbade its publication until after his death. Many thinkers have found his change of heart unconvincing, pointing out that he never apologized for his earlier statements. Some have gone as far as finding his whole work permeated by Nazi ideology and demanding the withdrawal of his works from the philosophy shelves of bookshops and libraries.

Heidegger's use of language was highly personal and difficult. Words change their meanings as time progresses; Heidegger often used words in an old-fashioned sense. He frequently made up new compound words. He used modern technical terms in a very broad and general sense; he frequently used puns and employed the same word to suggest different meanings. The topics he covered included logic, metaphysics, philosophy of history and of science, language, poetry, technology, Greek thought and mathematics. He felt that modern society has promoted and entrusted too much to technology. Our civilization has 'fallen out of Being'. We have forgotten Being. Heidegger stressed over and over again that we live in the presence of the fundamental mystery of existence; this is something which cannot be explained, but which, through hard thought and perseverance, we might come to appreciate.

---

**Timeline**

1889  Birth of Martin Heidegger in Baden, Germany
1913  First volume of Proust's *Remembrance of Things Past*
1914–18  First World War
            Heidegger's doctoral thesis in philosophy at the University
            of Freiburg
1915–23  Lectures at both Freiburg and Marburg universities
1917  Russian Revolution

1921   Publication of Wittgenstein's *Tractatus Logico-Philosophicus*
1927   Publication of Heidegger's *Being and Time*
1933   Hitler becomes German Chancellor
1933   Heidegger becomes Rector of the University of Freiburg and
         allies himself with Nazism
1934   Heidegger resigns the rectorship and withdraws into isolation
1936–39   Spanish Civil War
1939–45   Second World War
1947   Marshall Plan (American aid to war-ravaged countries of
         Europe)
1961   J. F. Kennedy President of the USA
1962–65   Second Vatican Council
1976   Death of Heidegger

## Thought

### Phenomenology

Heidegger early on followed the thought of his teacher Husserl (1859–1938). For Husserl, consciousness can concentrate and purify itself so that it perceives things as they are, before the distortions of interpretation or language. To help this process along Husserl had invented what he called phenomenology or phenomenological analysis, the abstract analysis of consciousness, and Heidegger took it up.

Phenomenology had proposed a theory of thinking consciousness; Heidegger went a step further and proposed a theory of Being. Phenomenology had proposed a description of the contents of consciousness; Heidegger proposed an interpretation of the contents of existence: plunging into the carefully hidden, mysterious operations of Being.

A page of Heidegger is almost impossible to read. Many people, professional philosophers among them, have wondered if he is being obscure on purpose so as to keep his thought safe among the privileged few who are initiated into its mysteries. But Heidegger is also thinking in ways that no philosopher of the Western tradition had ever thought before, and to express this new way of thinking he needed a new language – it cannot be expressed in everyday speech. Heidegger thus invented a new technical way of expressing himself, rather as modern scientists have constantly to invent new technical terms to convey the complexities of contemporary scientific thought. It is a language for philosophical specialists.

## Being

The earliest philosophers had asked: 'What is Being?' How do we now answer the question? We can't, said Heidegger; but what is worse we no longer ask this type of question; we don't even understand what it means.

Firstly, what is the difference between Being and a being? Everything which exists is a being: this book, the fire, the chair on which I am sitting, the desk in front of me, the wind outside, not forgetting myself. Now make a distinction between all these beings and what they are busy doing: they are busy . . . being. This business of 'being', is an action which is not exactly an action, is a state which is not exactly a state, it is more foundational than all that. It is Being. Being is not *a* being, it is the fact that there are beings; it is whatever causes beings to be.

And we still don't really know what Being is. It is more fundamental than the sense of 'is' and 'are' in the sentence: 'There are no cheques in my chequebook, but there is money on the bedside table.'

Just think of the world as it is, then try to imagine it without the Eiffel Tower. (That's easy!) Then try to imagine the world without architecture, then without dogs . . . Each time we take such a step we get closer to Nothing, a state where no thing exists, not even space and time. Not even anybody to imagine nothing. It requires a leap of the imagination to imagine Nothing. A similar leap of the imagination is required to get an idea of Being, what makes everything possible.

Heidegger is asking us to be attentive to Being, to what it is that causes beings to be. And by this he doesn't mean a primitive notion of

God: God brought in to wave a wand and make everything all right. He is asking us to feel our way into the meaning of Being as something profoundly different from the meaning of a bottle, a storm or a passport (and remember that a passport is more than an official document; it is function and possibility and limitation and identity). As beings we have a relationship with Being that we ought to explore.

People have forgotten Being. They have forgotten to wonder what Being is. We have been too busy developing a science fixated on beings.

## Dasein

*Dasein* is our 'thrown-ness'. Every one of us is thrown into our social environment. Our social environment is like a straitjacket thrown around us. When their environment moulds young persons so that they tend to act, react in a certain way, this becomes a *Dasein*. The way each *Dasein* has of existing is called *being-in-the-world*. *Dasein* is the structures of the contact of the human with Being. The fundamental existential structures are time, death and anxiety.

But a *Dasein* does not exist as an inert being (books, tables, tools); the characteristic of a *Dasein* is that 'there is Being'. Put another way, a *Dasein* is a 'being for whom there is Being'. A *Dasein* does not have possibilities (like a book which can be read or used as a doorstop, or a table which can be used for a meal, for study or even draped with sheets beneath which children can crawl into a private play-space); a *Dasein is* its own possibilities. The difference here is that the way the table is used depends upon the decision of the waiter, the student or the child. The table has no say in it. But each *Dasein* can decide for itself what it is going to be: shall I work in an office like my father, or shall I make up my own mind, grasp my own opportunities and be ME? Nothing is predetermined; a *Dasein* is not locked into an essence. A *Dasein*'s mode of being is openness to Being. A *Dasein* must create its own meaning.

*Dasein* is openness to Being and at the same time a factual element in the material world like any other being. A *Dasein* can interpret and understand Being, but the way it relates to being is in place before it starts to reflect or theorize. The first thing we must investigate and interpret is our being-in-the-world.

*Transcending our existence*

Our being-in-the-world is not just inert. (i.e., passive). We engage with the world, reach out to it. 'Exist', says Heidegger, is '*ex*-ist', to stand outside oneself. *Dasein* is 'being-with', being present in the world, in the presence of other transcendent presences in the world.

But the danger we face is a sort of *everydayness*; the danger that the thousand and one cares and little things that we have to deal with in our daily living will take us over. We are in danger of being reduced to the status of utensil. A tool, a utensil, has meaning only if people use it for their own ends. *Everydayness* is the tapestry of events that tends to reduce us to utensil status, impoverishing our openness to Being, locking us into limited horizons, reducing possibilities, being absorbed into the status of a being, losing the meaning of our own being.

*Dasein* can only be itself as it projects itself out into its possibilities.

So basically, either I have a mode of existence in which I never think about what I am or what I am doing, a completely unexamined mode of existence, or I can choose a mode of existence consciously allowing others to make all the decisions, or I can choose a mode of existence in which I assume responsibility for my own life.

---

**Being and Time (1927)**

- The world is a region of human concern. We are beings-in-the-world. When we participate and are involved in the world then the world becomes constitutive of human being.
- We have being in an environment, and share this world with others.
- We are creatures of concerns: our concerns are practical when they relate to the environment; they are personal when they relate to the community.

- The three fundamental characteristics of being human are

  1. Factuality: we are involved in the world;
  2. Existentiality: we are both project and possibility; this involves what we have been and also what we may become;
  3. Fallenness: we are in danger of becoming nothing more than a presence in the world, failing to make the most of our possibilities.

- Through anxiety we encounter nothingness, become aware of finitude and the necessity of death. Through resolution, and as we move through time, we appraise ourselves, choose with the wholeness of our being and achieve authentic existence.

### Time and authenticity

We are always preoccupied with something; we don't have a minute to think. Perhaps we would prefer not to. Very often, Heidegger says, this attitude reassures us; it absorbs us with beings. But this is a flight into being and away from Being, into the awareness of the emptiness of being, eventually causing *anguish*. It is when we confront *anguish* that we are given the opportunity to take a step back and redirect ourselves towards *authenticity*. 'Who am I?' 'Where am I going?' 'Why?' may be the questions of *anguish*, but they are also the questions that lead to the *authenticity* of *Dasein*.

All beings exist in time; time regulates them. *Dasein* is engaged in time. *Dasein* is what *Dasein* decides to be, is what *Dasein* does with its time. This particular mode of being in time causes *Dasein* to stand in a particular relationship with death. *Dasein* is the only being to be conscious that it is; the price to pay is that *Dasein* stands in consciousness of its death.

But *Dasein* can grab hold of itself and assume its own being, its possibility; here *Dasein* ceases to flee from itself and takes responsibility for its plans, its cares, its existence in time.

## *The human in technical mode*

Our preoccupations are functional; we tend to approach everything around us by seeking to appraise its value as resource, as means, as utensil. We are permanently in technical mode. This being in technical mode is, for Heidegger, a disastrous consequence of the forgetting of Being. Throughout human history we have concentrated on exploiting, on using beings (at first sticks, bones, stones; later weapons, machines, technology and now computers).

But Heidegger sees our technical mastery as spiralling out of control: we first used resources in accordance with nature; we now use resources to dominate nature. Technical mode started as a possible way of existing alongside beings, even though it involved a veiling of Being. Modern living involves the hegemony of the technical; all other possibilities are hidden by this all-powerfulness of the technical.

'Science', said Heidegger, 'does not think.' Science has to do with the manipulation of beings, and not with the revelation or the interpretation of Being. We have become the masters and possessors of nature. The world is a set of objects to manipulate; our art is how to calculate the best way of doing it. But thought is different from calculating, from devising ever more effective utensils. Thought is stopping still, realizing where we are and seeking an authenticity masked from us by *everydayness*. Thought meditates; the technical calculates.

## *Beyond metaphysics*

Heidegger thinks of openness (the gift of presence which is the kernel of being) as dynamic, willed action on the part of Being. 'Being gives itself.' Our consciousness is no longer encountering being; the stress has changed from *Dasein* to Being. I no longer bend my thought to what is; Being itself reaches out for the bent of my thinking.

---

**Metaphysics** is the study of being as being; speculation about the meaning of what is; the study of first principles and first causes; the rational knowledge of those realities that go beyond us; the rational study of things in themselves.

When metaphysics examines beings rather than Being, Being is hidden and reveals itself as beings. By going beyond metaphysics, by bending one's thoughts in such a way as to understand one's nature and take up those very questions, but on another level, the level that metaphysics wished to achieve before going so disastrously wrong on the journey, Being is unveiled to us.

As he reread the old metaphysical texts Heidegger continually focused on the hidden – revealing, on the veiling – unveiling, action of Being. Thus the history of Being is the way Being remained hidden for Plato, Aristotle, Descartes, Nietzsche, etc.

## Language and poetry

Being does not reveal itself because we speak and possess language. Rather Being reveals itself as 'speech'. 'Language is the house of Being', said Heidegger. Thought can merely say what comes from Being, but only says it at the very frontiers of the unsayable.

We do not arrive at the understanding of Being by mastery, by the technical perfection and adequacy of our language; we construct a habitable universe, in and out of the *building* of poetry.

What might be called a 'common-sense attitude to life' is one which remains on the surface, manipulating beings in a *busyness* which has no meaning, depth or significance. It is in the *building* of poetry that truth is allowed to shine.

## Appraisal

Phenomenology looks at the relationship between the world and the senses that experience the world, focusing on consciousness rather than on the unconscious. This detailed analysis/description of the world and our place in it was elaborated to help people see both harmful and positive ways of apprehending the world.

Heidegger is frequently classified as an 'existentialist philosopher', a description he vigorously rejected. He shifted the emphasis of thinkers from 'consciousness' to 'Being'. That is to say, instead of concentrating on how we are aware of what is there, we should concentrate on what *is* there. The whole philosophical tradition of ideas about what is there interferes with our ability to appreciate Being.

The very fact that things, including us, are there is in itself wonderful and incomprehensible. But the tradition has always sought to explain it. We have to be able to see past the tradition of explanations in order to see Being for what it is. This has more to do with wonder than with rational examination.

Heidegger's aim was to bring about an analysis through which Being shows itself, but he really never got beyond a phenomenological analysis of what it is to be human. It is not always clear what he meant by Being, or why our forgetting of Being is a problem.

What do you now understand by Being? Would you rather forget about it? Why? Would you consider Being to be something about which we may not speak and, if so, why? Even if it is difficult to talk about, is Being a legitimate subject of concern and enquiry?

We cannot separate knowledge from experience; they are part of the same reality. We do not necessarily develop attitudes about our lives because we think about them. Authenticity is refusing to take things for granted, refusing to accept that things might already be figured out and delivered to us. It is important for us to be involved in the decisions of our lives and of the world around us.

Existence is everything; nothing can lie outside it. Being takes place in time. Times change, we need to work with these changes and make the most of new possibilities. There is no explanation for life until we decide what explanations to believe in. We all individually have to work out what to do with our lives and try out new possibilities, be aware of new possibilities and of course of their limitations. We have to do this now; time presses on. This suggests an ethic, but Heidegger did not develop an ethic. What sort of ethic do notions such as authentic and inauthentic living suggest?

Heidegger's admirers praise the relentless determination of his analysis, the dignity and serenity of his exercise of thinking. He understood the manifestation of Being as word. The task of the philosopher was to hear and understand that word. Yet he appears as a promoter of the *arcanum*, and that is a position which attracts ridicule in the philosophical world.

> **Arcanum** is the closed circle of the few who promote mysterious or obscure understanding.

Heidegger has been severely criticized, and indeed deserves severe criticism, for the way he philosophized. His language appears deliberately obscure, whereas the philosophical tradition seeks to *make clear*. Increasingly after his resignation Heidegger philosophized in private to small elite groups of initiates. But is philosophy not a public questioning for all?

There remains his ambiguous relationship with the Nazi enterprise. In 1933 he took an important university post which he used to commend Nazi ideology unambiguously to his students and colleagues as 'the present and future German reality and its rule'. In seeking to ally his thought with Nazism he may have been making what he saw as a shrewd career move, though ultimately it was not. Nevertheless his thought is not easily tied to ideology and is in fact thought without a body of epistemological, political or moral teaching. Less harsh critics point out that he resigned his post ten months later and that he did not play an active part in Nazi atrocities. However, he did not denounce them. Neither did he later apologize for his past words; he merely said he would no longer write thus and in retrospect would not have done so in 1934. Nonetheless, unsympathetic critics accuse him of active and conscious complicity in crimes against humanity.

# 14 Jean-Paul Sartre: Existentialist Anguish

Existentialism is a recognized form of metaphysics, and it received its most popular form of expression with Jean-Paul Sartre. Sartre was known as 'the pope of existentialism' and had a huge influence and an enormous popular following. Many have remarked that existentialism, after the Second World War, was less an academic discipline and more of a mood, practised less in the academy and talked about more in the cellars of St Germain des Prés. Indeed, 'existentialist' was at one stage used to cover everything from the latest song to the latest dress fashion. Sartre's philosophical works *Being and Nothingness* and *Critique of Dialectical Reason* can be extremely technical and dense, and quite unappealing to the general reader. (The *Critique* has even been described as 'a monster of unreadability'). He also published a number of novels (such as *Nausea* and *The Roads to Freedom*) and plays (*The Flies, In Camera*),

Jean-Paul Sartre

which caused the ordinary reader to be aware of the sort of things that existentialism discussed. He is held by many to be a very fine dramatic author.


## Life


Sartre was born in Paris in 1905. His father died early. Jean-Paul was brought up by his mother and her family, who came from Alsace. His grandfather ran a language school and was distantly related to Albert Schweitzer.

Sartre attended the Ecole normale supérieure from 1924 to 1928. Here he met Simone de Beauvoir who was to become his life-long companion, support, collaborator and 'soul-friend' (though they would never have used such a term). Simone de Beauvoir has left us an account of what it was like to sit for the *agrégation* (an elite competitive exam). Students with thermos flasks and biscuits crowded into the hall, a supervisor placed his hand in an urn and drew out a slip of paper. He announced the subject: 'Liberty and contingency'. That was it; there was no choice. A single exam session could last up to five hours. *Agrégés*, as those holding the *agrégation* are called, have a right to a post in a lycée or university. They have very few teaching hours and are expected to do research and write.

When Sartre obtained his *agrégation* he taught in Le Havre and Laon. He was later moved to Paris. From 1933 to 1935 he was a research student in Germany. He then returned to teach once more in Paris, in the Lycée Condorcet. At the outbreak of the war he was drafted into the French army's meteorological service. He was captured during the rout of the Allied forces in 1940 and released in 1941. He returned to teaching and was later involved in the French Resistance. He and his companions had a gut hatred of fascism.

After the war he played a leading role in founding and editing *Les Temps modernes*, a monthly review devoted to socialist and existentialist matters (it still exists). He flirted with communism but never joined the Communist Party. He abandoned any attempt to ally communism and existentialism. They were mutually incompatible. His most striking act of independence, refusing to fit into any preconceived mould, was his rejection of the Nobel Prize for Literature, awarded to him in 1964. His outlook was what the French are likely to call *gauchiste*. This is a rather informal collection of radical outlooks, always aspiring to be more radical still. *Gauchisme* does not appear to have any coherent programme for government other than to be against it. Sartre was prominent in the 'theoretical' talks held in the great lecture hall of the Sorbonne which debated the events of the students' revolt of 1968. He was fundamentally opposed to General de Gaulle and the policies he stood for during his period of power from 1958 until 1969. De Gaulle recognized Sartre's popularity and influence. 'On n'arrête pas Voltaire' 'You don't arrest Voltaire', he is supposed to have snapped at a government minister who wanted Sartre arrested for promoting civil disobedience.

Sartre and de Beauvoir lived publicly, that is to say all aspects of their lives were commented upon and described by them in their own works: technical, fictional and autobiographical. His political work was a source of great disappointment to him and the causes he promoted did not prosper. His eyesight deteriorated greatly towards the end of his life. He died in 1980, age probably being a factor, but aggravated by abuse of prescription drugs. He never held a university post and he never married. It is said that he did once offer to marry de Beauvoir, but she refused indignantly to be associated with such a middle-class institution as marriage.

---

**Timeline**

1905  Birth of Jean-Paul Sartre
1910  Bertrand Russell's and A.N. Whitehead's *Principia Mathematica*
1914–18  First World War
1916  Einstein's Theory of General Relativity
1917  Russian Revolution

1920  Congress of Tours and formation of the French Communist
           Party
1924  Sartre attends the École normale supérieure; meets Simone de
           Beauvoir
1928  Sartre awarded *agrégation*; starts teaching career
1933–35  Research student in Germany
1936–39  Spanish Civil War
1937–38  Stalinist purges in Russia
1938  Publication of *Nausea* (*La Nausée*) his first novel
1939  Publication of *Le Mur*, collection of short stories
1939  Sartre called up to the French army
1940  Fall of France; Sartre prisoner of war
1941  Sartre released; resumes teaching career; joins French
           Resistance
1943  Publication of *Being and Nothingness* (*L'Etre et le néant*);
           presentation of *The Flies*
1944  Presentation of *In Camera* (considered his masterpiece)
1945  Edits *Les Temps modernes*; abandons teaching to write
           fulltime
1947–49  *Situations*, essays in three volumes
1948  Publication of *What is Literature?*
1958  Algerian crisis; de Gaulle returns to power
1960  Publication of *Critique of Dialectical Reason*
1964  Publication of autobiography, *Words*
1968  Student crisis in France; Sartre increasingly involved in radical
           politics
1980  Death of Jean-Paul Sartre

**Phenomenal** refers (in philosophical usage) to things and events perceived through the senses.

**Perspective** refers to how aspects of a subject relate to each other, the point of view from which we examine objects and themes.

> **Contingent** means not necessary, happening by chance or accident, dependent upon other conditions or events.
>
> **Metaphysics** is the study of being as being; speculation about the meaning of what is; the study of first principles and first causes; the rational knowledge of those realities that go beyond us; the rational study of things in themselves.

## Thought

### *What is existentialism?*

Existentialism is a movement of revolt, such as happens from time to time, against over-systematization in philosophy. The existentialist current of thought is traced back to the Danish thinker Kierkegaard, continuing with Nietzsche (who had never heard of Kierkegaard), Jaspers and Heidegger (who denied angrily that he was an existentialist).

Existentialism is a current of thought that believes that *existence* comes before *essence*. To illustrate this, Sartre asks us to consider a paperknife. It is a product made by an artisan. This artisan had an idea of the knife before he made it; he knew why he wanted to make it and how he wanted to use it; he had worked out how to go about manufacturing it. In this way the essence of the paperknife (ideas about what it was for and how it should look and be made) preceded the actual making of the paperknife, its existence. So from this point of view *essence* preceded *existence*.

If we think about the human person and have an idea of God, it is of a God who, when creating, knows precisely what is being created. The idea, the master-plan, came first in the mind of God: *essence* preceded *existence*.

Even when we come to eighteenth-century atheism, the Enlightenment thinkers simply suppressed the idea of God, but kept an idea of human nature: each individual is a particular example of a universal master-plan of what human beings are supposed to be like.

*Essence* still preceded *existence*. But Sartre declared that as God does not exist, there can be no master-plan; but there is at least one being whose existence has to come before its essence and that is the human being.

For Sartre, *existence* precedes *essence*. 'We mean that man first of all exists, encounters himself, surges up in the world – and defines himself afterwards.' Human beings are nothing; there is no preordained plan of what they ought to be. They will not be anything until later, and then they will be what they make of themselves.

This is not a critique of how we know, what we can know. This is a hard look at what it means to be human and to ask what should one do, what can one do, and what will one later become? It is not part of a philosophical outlook which concentrates on the question, 'How do we know?'

---

### Being and Nothingness (1943)

- Being is never exhausted by any of its phenomenal aspects: no particular perspective reveals the entire character of being.
- Being-in-itself (*en-soi*) is fixed, complete, wholly given, absolutely contingent, with no reason for its being. It is more or less equivalent to the inert world of objects and things.
- Being-for-itself (*pour-soi*) is incomplete, indeterminate, fluid. It is the being of human consciousness.
- Being-in-itself is prior to being-for-itself. Being-for-itself is dependent upon being-in-itself for its origin. Being-for-itself is derived from being-in-itself by an act of nihilation.
- Freedom is the heart of the human; in anxiety humans become aware of their freedom, know themselves to be responsible for their own being by commitment, seek the impossible reunion with being-in-itself, in despair know themselves to be forever at odds with the 'others' who, even by their glances, can threaten an individual, turning him into an object.

## Atheism and values

Sartre's existentialism has one underlying assumption. This assumption appears to him to be self-evident: God does not exist. The existence of humans excludes the existence of God. There is no such thing as pre-existing human nature. Humans are the future of humans; humans are what they make of themselves. Thus existentialism is a humanism.

Sartre usually mocks all attempts to defend humanist values, because they assume a pre-existent human nature. But humans are responsible. They are condemned to be free. We cannot pose the problem of what it is like to be a human being in the abstract. We must work out our being in concrete situations. We are involved in given situations; we cannot claim to be unavailable for involvement. This obliges us to make choices, but it is also the basis of our liberty.

Workers mould their material, shape it to their ends. Humans, by their actions, mould the reality they are confronted with. An *authentic act* is when individuals take responsibility for the situations in which they find themselves and by action go beyond it. Only our actions have any value. Once we act that action cannot be reversed: that action judges us, good intentions cannot be appealed to, nor can we appeal to any notions that we form about ourselves, about what we are like. An appeal to such things is *bad faith*.

This philosophy is based on action. Nevertheless our awareness of ourselves is founded on an experience of the *absurdity* of existence. We are contingent beings, there is no reason why we should exist. As soon as we seek to involve ourselves in authentic action, what do we base our choices on? What are the criteria for authentic actions? There are none; Sartre rejects traditional values. He rejects notions of 'good' or 'evil' as absolute values (existence precedes essence).

All I have to go on is my freedom. Yet as soon as I make a decision my decision impinges on other people, I affect their freedom. The tension between the necessity for action, of having no value to base my action on and the inevitability that my freedom limits the freedom of others all produce *anguish*. 'Man is a useless passion.'

*'Man is condemned to be free'*

In his play *The Flies* Sartre retells the story of Orestes. When Agamemnon returned victorious from the war against Troy, he was murdered by his wife Clytemnestra. Her lover Aegisthus became king in his place. Electra and Orestes, daughter and son respectively of Clytemnestra and Agamemnon, must avenge their father by killing their mother and thus ridding the city of the plague of flies. Electra persuades Orestes to act.

For Sartre, the action of Orestes is the symbol of a human freedom which is incompatible with the existence of God. Such freedom is expressed by an authentic act, taking responsibility for the situation in which he finds himself and acting without reference to traditional notions of good or evil. The Furies, the avenging goddesses, will track Orestes down; yet is he not victorious nonetheless? During the play Jupiter tells Aegisthus that once freedom has exploded within a human soul, even the gods can do nothing to that man; human beings are free, even though they do not realize it.

The play is also interesting because it was first presented during the Nazi occupation of France. It managed to avoid Nazi censorship because the censors read it as the reworking of an old Greek myth. The spectators read it as speaking passionately to their actual (unfree) political situation.

*Sartre's ethics*

While Sartre was perfectly capable of writing abstract tomes in philosophical jargon, 'monsters of unreadability', he often worked out philosophical difficulties, or rather posed philosophical dilemmas, by telling stories, or writing plays. And he wrote extremely well. So instead of reading about the 'theory' of ethics, we might consider a story Sartre told to get the feel of the problem. (We remind ourselves that ethics is the study of the principles governing what is right or wrong and is concerned with notions such as 'good', 'obligation' and 'duty'.) Here is the story:

It was during the occupation of France by the Nazis during the Second World War. A young man was looking for advice from Sartre about what he should do. His elder brother had been killed during the earlier fighting; his father was on bad terms with his mother and had in any case a tendency to collaborate with the occupying power. The young man wanted to go to England to join the Free French forces. To do this he would have to leave his mother behind. She would be alone, unprotected, already upset by her husband's betrayal and even more distressed if her only remaining child should leave, for he was now her only moral and material support.

What should he do? And what should help him choose? Christian doctrine said, love your neighbour, choose the more difficult path, but did not tell him which was the more difficult path or which was the neighbour he should love – the fighting men abroad or his mother.

Values are vague. All he could trust was his instincts. In the end feeling was what counted. He could only choose what pushed him more in one direction. If he felt he loved his mother more then he ought to sacrifice all else for her. If his love for his mother was not enough then he would choose to go.

The 'hero' of the tale is concerned with freedom and self-honesty. Sartre's point was that there are no moral laws, principles like love are not capable of helping us to make decisions, each moral decision can only be made by the individual concerned and that individual can only make it for himself and for nobody else. But the problem is that such an outlook can justify any action regardless of its effect on other people. This illustrates not only the freedom but also the anguish.

## 'Hell is other people'

Sartre's play *In Camera* gives us a glimpse of how he viewed the human condition. It should be pointed out that, when he speaks of hell, this is not a theological place of eternal punishment: God does not exist; there is neither heaven nor hell. Hell in this world is living under the gaze of others: being judged by others, having to take others into account.

Garcin (the coward who thought he was a hero), Estelle (the child-murderer, who is also responsible for the death of her lover) and Inez (who hates men and, what is more, needs to see others suffer in order to exist) have all died and are locked together in the same room. They begin by not telling the truth about themselves, building themselves up to be better than they are, but soon their failings become evident and they torment each other. They can never be alone. They will always have to take account of each other. 'Hell is other people!'

## Existentialism and literature

Sartre was a strong personality who exerted considerable influence on the period immediately after the Second World War. It is not always easy to distinguish in his fictional and dramatic writings what belongs to his philosophical convictions, what to outside influences (he was a great admirer of the contemporary American novel), and what is derived from his own personality. His philosophical thought becomes clearer as we read his literary work and his philosophical thought inspires and enlivens those works. His literary writing deals directly with the social problems of the time and literature's links with life are strengthened.

But Sartre also used the writings of others to illustrate his ideas; he was in fact a sharp literary critic and published studies on a number of writers. His study of Baudelaire appeared in 1947, on Jean Genet in 1952 and on Flaubert in 1971–72. *What is Literature?* (1948) is a fine collection of important literary comment.

## Sartre and his times

In his later years Sartre became quite sceptical about the power of literature, but remained aware of philosophical currents; he was above all aware of criticism directed against the extreme subjectivism of existentialism. The last years of his life were devoted to radical politics and he edited left-wing papers and reviews such as *La cause du peuple* and *Libération*. He supported anything that challenged authority. When *La cause du peuple* was censored, he defied the order by selling it himself in the streets of Paris. The communists were long-time ideological enemies whom he never ceased to oppose. He continued to act in support of human rights throughout the world.


## Appraisal

With Jean-Paul Sartre we come face to face with a vision of what it is like to be a human being rather than a statement of how it is that we know or when we can say that we know.

It has been rightly said that existentialism is a mood, rather than a philosophy. However, if it is not a form of epistemology, it is a form of metaphysics.

Sartre witnessed the Second World War. He had been a prisoner of war. He considered himself, and the whole world with him, directly threatened by the cruelty of history, the concentration camps and the invention of nuclear weapons.

Sartre's vision of the world was dark. This return to barbarism led him, on behalf of the whole human race, to question the meaning of human destiny. He seemed to consider it his duty as a thinking person to submit the facts of existence to conscientious, vigilant and lucid criticism in order to highlight what is tragic and absurd. His work was in fact a long moral reflection on his times, the affirmation of a metaphysical scandal. Would your reflection on the world in which you live lead you to affirm a metaphysical scandal, or would you be more optimistic? Would this reflection nudge you towards activism or acceptance? Are there any grounds for hope?

Sartre's work is not rigorous. His postulate that there is no God remains just that: a postulate. Sartre accepts it as self-evident and in his thought everything flows from it. Can the categorical rejection of God be proved more easily than the existence of God? Would you say that Sartre's sense of a world deserted by transcendence and emptied of all necessity, into which the human being is thrown out, abandoned, is a disposition or a fact?

## 15  Jacques Derrida: Deconstructing Reality

In Derrida we come to a most interesting and controversial philosopher of language; or is it a philosopher of meaning, or of text? Some say he was the greatest philosopher of his generation; others claim that people only say that because no one understands him. Booksellers are never sure on which shelf to place his books or books about him: should it be philosophy or literary criticism? It is said that his earliest ambition was to become a professional footballer. His great insights include the notion that whenever language expresses an idea it changes it. Furthermore, any text will at some stage say the opposite to what it appears to be saying and produce a multitude of diverse meanings.

Some people say that Derrida was not really a philosopher at all. Others argue that he performed the most vital of all philosophical services: he brought a critical spirit to bear on whatever he turned his attention to.

Jacques Derrida

## Life

Jacques Derrida was born in 1930, near the city of Algiers. Algeria was at that time a French colony, and during the Second World War was ruled from Vichy France. Because of the regime's anti-Semitic laws the young Jacques Derrida, being Jewish, was excluded from the education system.

Following rather disrupted secondary studies, Derrida went to mainland France in 1949 and eventually enrolled at the Ecole normale supérieure, where he studied philosophy. At first he enthusiastically embraced the existentialist philosophy of Jean-Paul Sartre. (He always read widely: Kierkegaard, Heidegger, Joyce.) He was awarded the *agrégation*\* in 1957, the year he married Marguerite Aucouturier. Derrida did his military service during the Algerian war, not as a combatant but in the army's education service.

Derrida was invited back to the Ecole normale supérieure as an assistant. During the 1960s and 1970s he published a number of books and articles which made his reputation as a post-structuralist thinker. His first three books, *Writing and Difference, Speech and Phenomena* and *Of Grammatology* were all published in 1967, but he did not present his doctoral thesis to the Sorbonne until 1984. He gave seminars at the University of Berlin, was particularly welcome in America, taught at Johns Hopkins University (Baltimore) and later at the University of California at Irvine. He also taught at the prestigious Collège de France.

French universities, however, remained suspicious of Derrida. So too did Cambridge University, where the proposal to grant him an honorary doctorate was forced to a vote in 1992. Derrida was given his degree by 336 votes to 204. Other universities all over the world have been more openhearted.

Serious newspapers and journals were publishing articles about Derrida by the early 1970s. He was interested in literary theory, but had a serious disagreement with Philippe Sollers and the *Tel Quel*

---

\* The *agrégation* is the French qualification conferring the right to teach in a secondary school or university.

group of literary theorists. Derrida's wife had family connections in Czechoslovakia (as it then was) and consequently in the 1980s he founded the Jan Hus Association to help dissident and persecuted Czech intellectuals. He was imprisoned in Prague following an illegal conference and was only released as a result of vigorous intervention by the French President, François Mitterrand. He later became interested in the science park at La Villette on the outskirts of Paris and wrote about architecture. He was also involved with Palestinian intellectuals in the Occupied Territories.

Derrida's main works include *Of Grammatology* (1967), *Writing and Difference* (1967), *Margins of Philosophy* (1972), *Dissemination* (1972), *The Truth in Painting* (1978), *Memoirs of the Blind* (1990), and *Spectres of Marx* (1993).

In 1992 Derrida was awarded the French Legion of Honour. He died in 2004.

---

## Timeline

1916  Ferdinand de Saussure's *Course in General Linguistics*

1930  Birth of Jacques Derrida

1933  Hitler becomes Chancellor

1936–39  Spanish Civil War

1937–38  Purges in the USSR

1939–45  Second World War

1940  Fall of France; Derrida excluded from the educational system
         Derrida arrives in mainland France

1954  Fall of Dien Bien Phu; start of war in Algeria

1957  Derrida gains agrégation; marries Marguerite Aucouturier

1957  Roland Barthes' *Mythologies*

1967  Derrida publishes *Of Grammatology, Writing and Difference*
         and *Speech and Phenomena*

1968  Student uprising in France

1969  First man on the moon

1976–84  Michel Foucault's *The History of Sexuality*
1979  Jean-François Lyotard invents term 'postmodern'
1984  Derrida defends his doctoral thesis at the Sorbonne
1992  Derrida awarded Legion of Honour
         Creation of the European Union
2004  Death of Jacques Derrida

## Thought

### Structuralism

Structuralism is a philosophical and methodological outlook which was fashionable in the 1960s. It is a method of studying language, society and the works of artists and novelists. Its main teaching is that reality is composed of relationships rather than things. According to structuralists, when we see, feel, smell, consider any object, it is there in so far as we perceive it, but it is also not there in so far as its reality is also composed of its relation to 'the whole system', a whole web of relationships existing at any given time and of which each percipient could not be aware.

This outlook developed from the work of Ferdinand de Saussure (1857–1913), a Swiss linguist who changed the study of linguistics from a diachronic to a synchronic discipline. That is to say he taught that scholars should concentrate less on the historical development of language and more on how the elements fit together at one given time to allow language to function at that moment. His ground-breaking lectures were delivered from 1907 to 1911. His *Course in General Linguistics* was published posthumously in 1916, having been reconstituted from a student's notes.

Structuralism tends to divide our perception of the world into binary categories, minimal pairs: good/bad, right/wrong, cooked/raw, true/untrue, male/female, light/dark, left/right, fact/fiction, nature/nurture, etc. It analyses the structures that lie behind or beneath things. It tends to distrust history and concentrates instead on the web of patterns holding at any given time. Derrida reacted against this outlook.

## Logocentric prejudice

Derrida believed that the great minds of Western civilization had a distorting bias in all their thought and writing. This was a bias in favour of speech and against writing. He called this type of writing 'logocentric' and claimed that it was in need of 'deconstruction'.

Put very crudely, logocentrism is the idea that we can get to the very essence of meaning when we succeed in choosing the right word for the idea. If we speak we are at one remove from an idea, if we write we are at two removes from an idea, so speech is prioritized over writing, because here we are closer to the essence of meaning. Such fixed meanings can be known with certainty through the use of human reason. This was the idea that Derrida was attacking.

Derrida also believed that the desire for certainty had held Western intellectual life and thought in a tyrannical grip by excluding everything that cannot be known with certainty. This has at times included poetry, ethics and mysticism. Derrida alleged that such an attitude was part of the tyranny of logocentrism.

Socrates, he claimed, had refused to write anything down on the grounds that philosophy is to be the living encounter between thinking people; this was also why Plato had written his works as 'dialogues'. Aristotle had said that thoughts in the mind are in direct contact with things; speech is a sign, at one remove from our thought, writing is a sign of a sign, one remove further from thought and contact with things. Priests and scribes acquired power at the expense of ordinary people, because they controlled law, records and language through writing, thus leading to a form of dishonesty. Later thinkers saw learning to read and write as a form of liberation, as taking control of one's own destiny.

Modern people think that if we don't have a word for something it doesn't exist. A word is necessary to perceive a thing as it is. Controlling language is controlling things. What is more, logocentrism tends to give greater value to one of the two poles of binary opposites: light over dark, fact over fiction, cooked over raw, male over female, capital over labour, and occasionally indeed, the other way around.

Logocentrism occurs when we give the spoken word more importance than the written word. Speaking is a sign of presence. When we speak to somebody they are with us. Writing is a sign of absence. We write to somebody because they are at a remove. The more words are shut away in writing, logocentrism maintains, the more they are copies rather than the real thing.

Derrida attacked this theory of presence and origins by attacking the notion than speech has priority over writing. He was not making an historical claim here; he was not saying that our primitive ancestors could write before they could speak. He was saying that *both* forms of language are signs; both exhibit partial absence and partial presence, which is to say that both are relational.

He further noted, with an ironic smile, that all those who attack writing, complaining that it is derivative, do so by conducting their attacks in writing.

When Derrida attacked the priority of speech over writing, he was attacking the notion of any sort of absolute. Both speech and writing are signs. They are useful because they can be used over and over again; we never come close to an original presence or meaning. Thus language is a partial presence and a partial absence.

### *Différance*

In structural linguistics, meaning comes about because there is a difference between signs. If friends tell me they have a sore hip, I understand their meaning because I appreciate the difference (amongst others) between 'hip' and 'lip'. I do not go directly to a meaning, I distinguish between a set of possible relations. Derrida claimed that meaning is never immediate; it is always deferred.

But if we meet a situation where we cannot make binary decisions, then matters are undecidable and upset the established order. Horror films often make their play by upsetting the established order and causing chaos; they use a situation which does not fit our binary logic. Frankenstein is an example: neither man nor machine, human nor animal. Comfort is restored with the reinstatement of binary order. But what if this binary order cannot be recalled; what if undecidability is the norm?

Derrida claimed that undecidability is in fact an element of the philosophy of the Western tradition, but that the tradition refuses to recognize this basic fact. There are many words in the Western tradition that are ambiguous, can be interpreted in a good or bad sense. Texts frequently fail to note this ambiguity and so cut out one of the binary poles of meaning. In English 'drug' is an example; it has a use that suggests therapy and a use that suggests undisciplined abuse, even enforced narcotic 'absence'.

For Derrida, writing has qualities that disrupt structuralist opposites.

Words, are of course, never univocal. They never have one meaning and one meaning only, which is fixed and will never change. For instance, the word 'pen' can mean a writing instrument, a female swan, a small enclosure for animals; in the USA it is used as short for 'penitentiary' (a prison); in the Caribbean it can mean a cattle farm and also a fortified dock for submarines. The context will usually give us the sense.

However, some language differences are so subtle we slip from one to the other and back again without noticing. For instance:

> The end of a thing is its perfection. Death is the end of life, therefore death is the perfection of life.

In this saying 'end' is used in the sense of 'goal', but also in the sense of 'last event'. The argument seems to work only if we do not notice the two different meanings. When we do notice the two different meanings the argument does not make sense.

There are also metaphorical meanings. A metaphorical meaning is not the same as a literal meaning. One might say that teenagers need space. This could mean that teenagers need their own private rooms on which they impose their own stamp. But it could also mean that they need the freedom to try out their own ideas and develop their own creativity, the space to make mistakes.

All the above examples are now obvious. But we conduct our daily lives in a welter of such confusions and do not notice the 'slippage'.

Derrida stressed that there is a basic undecidability about language; it is part of its warp and woof. We can never get to final bedrock meaning. He 'deconstructed' all these uncertainties about language and showed up the quality of undecidability within which language operates.

Derrida's writings did not set out arguments of the conventional academic kind; they rather trawled through texts of Plato, Husserl or de Saussure, noting where undecidables were at work, where the text was unsure of itself. He claimed thus to be undermining the foundations of Western rationalist metaphysics.

---

**Metaphysics** is the study of being as being; speculation about the meaning of what is; the study of first principles and first causes; the rational knowledge of those realities that go beyond us; the rational study of things in themselves.

---

Once language enters the public domain, the speaker or writer loses control over it. Just think of the way a new book, a novel for instance, or a film or a song is understood or misunderstood, interpreted or misinterpreted by the reviewers immediately after it appears.

Finally, we are in a position to deal with '*différance*', a word which Derrida invented himself. The word '*différence*' exists in French and means difference, dissimilarity. The verb '*différer*', present participle '*différant*', means to put off, to delay. Out of these two words Derrida invented '*différance*'. This new word is intended to cover all the meanings which are left out by the fact that the word does not exist. '*Différence*' and '*Différance*' are pronounced in exactly the same way. You can only distinguish between them in writing.

This new word does not stand for a new concept; rather, it plays around the notion of undecidability. Language, thought and meaning are now all in an uncomfortable position; they are unstable. They force us to ask ourselves if language can be relied upon. A final decision on meaning will have to be postponed.

## Writing and 'iterability'

Most of us have a simple technique for dealing with words or sentences that could have several meanings. We try to put the word into context, but will context always be able to provide meaning? Laws, for instance, are passed with certain contexts in mind. But what might happen if a law, which is passed with one set of contexts in mind, has to be applied in a totally different situation that no legislator could have imagined?

Derrida thus saw writing as 'iterable': repeatable with difference. Writing is always eventually cut free from its sender and the person to whom it is addressed. It is then read, frequently with different results, by third parties for whom it could never have been intended.

Let us take an example: the case of Homer and the *Iliad*. Homer was the blind poet (thus the seer into the mysteries hidden from ordinary mortals with normal eyesight) of a now vanished civilization. The poem's ideas of right and wrong have to do with the 'heroic' concepts of a warrior class: honour, courage, etc. It was read, or more probably recited or sung, at the communal feastings of a society where most people could neither read nor write.

It is now read mostly in the centrally-heated studies of members of a privileged and classically educated social class; they all possess private homes and cars, and are conscious that any prospect of hostilities now could mean total war and complete annihilation.

The poem is no doubt read differently by those who see all motives as economic and who might see the overt reason for the war, the seduction of Helen, as a pretext for attacking and acquiring the wealth of a prosperous rival.

Feminists, for whom the notion of the 'possession' of a woman is intolerable, read it differently again.

How can the *Iliad* be read in 2006 CE in the same way it was read in 800 BCE?

## Literature is the very heart of deconstruction

Derrida insisted on the singularity of literary effort. He saw language being reinvented in every work as the writer progresses. So his readings of many writers involved an interest in the 'poet', the person struggling with the language in which the work is forged, but those same readings involve a theoretical reflection about what is happening in language. Language, for Derrida, is like a ghost. It is continually repeated as it is; it appears different on each occasion. Poets, writers, dramatists are repeatedly touched by the genius of language and in turn, repeatedly, affect it.

Derrida rethought the notion of 'text'. He came to see it as a series of traces which cannot be reduced to the very materiality of the resulting written object. Indeed we only have access to what is beyond language through this new notion of text. This is the meaning of his dictum: 'There is nothing outside the text.'

Derrida suggests that there are three types of 'signature':

(1) The name of the author on the page.
(2) The 'style', the singular features of the text: rhythm, length of phrase, choice of vocabulary.
(3) But for the 'signature' to work, it must be handed over in trust to the 'virtual reader' who now has the responsibility to receive and accept, to 'countersign' and to authenticate this message.

## Derrida and religion

When thinking about religion, Derrida stresses the necessity of a starting-point which is not that of a binary opposition: on the one hand religion, on the other hand reason and the sort of critique of religion made by Marx, Nietzsche or Freud, for example. He believed religion and reason have the same source: the notion of response.

Reason is always tempted to ignore the dimension of faith. Faith is always tempted because it is an impulse towards life (carrying notions of the holy, the saved, the pure, the clean), but also an impulse towards death (carrying the notion of sacrifice). It carries the sanction of the sacred. He invites all believers to meditate on the evils committed for the very reason that religion carries the notion of universal sacrifice.

The difficulty resides in the name 'God', particularly when we consider that God is what we are not: God is Other. Derrida locates this idea of Other in God's statement to Moses, 'I am that I am' in the episode of the burning bush (Exodus 3.14). Language began before us and without us, and that is where theologians locate God. Such a language is open to the notion of 'theological-becoming'. Religion is the fact of placing God in discourse, the coming of God into language. When we speak of language and of nothing being outside language, we have already been talking theology.

For Derrida, neither God nor religion is a stable concept and he often seems to avoid the notion of religion; his position *vis-à-vis* theology is not easily identified. He does, however, recognize the closeness of the act of thinking deconstruction and the act of thinking negative or apophatic theology.

---

**Apophatic (*via negativa*) theology** is a way of looking beyond all created categories of sensation to the God who cannot be thought. It is only within the darkness of faith, when intellectual and sense impressions have been stripped away, that the soul can get close to God. This *via negativa* moves towards God by asserting that the divine being is not any of the qualities that God is said to be. It is a form of mysticism.

---

On another front, Derrida has maintained that negative theology belongs in a space where its axioms would have to be questioned by deconstruction. Derrida was not a mystic: one who experiences the divine presence. But mysticism also bears witness to experiences of separation, detachment and abandonment. Derrida, though an atheist, recognized in his Jewish inheritance the experience of 'receiving' and of saying 'yes': of selecting, filtering, interpreting, transforming, de-forming what was received. Such acts are both faithful and transgressive.

## Deconstruction

Maybe we have now reached a stage where we can try to say what deconstruction is. It seems as if Derrida has been continually waging war against the whole Western tradition of the reign of reason, which he saw as a dishonest searching after certainty. Derrida has called it the 'logocentric quest': the search for the most appropriate and most correct word by which the inner thought is expressed: the word by which reason is made visible.

Logocentrism is looking for a totally rational language that perfectly represents the real world: the *presence* of the world, the *essence* in the word. Derrida pointed out that such a picture is in fact a tyranny that can only be realized by suppressing everything that is uncertain.

Indeed, for this very reason, certain thinkers have dogmatically excluded poetry (Plato), theology and ethics (Hume), art, religion, metaphysics and ethics (Wittgenstein) from what can be known, from what we are allowed to call knowledge, thus imposing a different form of thought control.

Meaning is not inherent in signs; it does not dwell behind the outward appearance of signs. Thinkers influenced by structural linguistics have consistently pointed out that meaning is the result of the relationships between signs. But Derrida went further: the structures of meaning must include the people who seek and create meaning. There is no rational vantage-point *outside* meaning from which we can assess it 'scientifically'. We, the seekers after meaning, are involved in the meanings *which we create*. When Derrida says, 'there is nothing outside the text', he means all practices of interpretation which we use. If I read the tale of *Little Red Riding Hood* and say that this is a cautionary tale which adults tell to children to frighten them away from dangerous places (the forest), my interpretation does not stand outside the text; it becomes part of the meaning of the text, whether or not the original tellers of the tale wanted it to be read thus.

## Appraisal

Deconstruction is the way Derrida unravelled how a text is constructed in order to reveal hidden meanings. Each text, said Derrida, has layers of meanings which have grown up as the text is read and reread in later historical settings and different cultural contexts.

It is believed that language systems are 'natural', but in fact they are constructs which can act as power systems which are often oppressive. Thus we must develop means of revealing different readings.

A text is not merely a piece of writing on the page; it is any construct held to carry meaning. It therefore includes interviews, conversations, paintings, pieces of music – they do not have to be written down. All these will eventually contradict themselves. If we minutely examine these contradictions we begin to spot the ways in which the 'reader' is being manipulated, by the 'author' or the 'text'.

Every reader of a text approaches a text with certain assumptions; these are as important as what the 'author' 'says' in the text. They also imply meaning. So no text has a stable meaning. The assumptions and meanings that I bring to a given text are different from the assumptions and meanings which you bring to the same text. And the readings of the text will depend on multiple contexts.

One highly significant aspect of Derrida's writings is that they seem to undermine the possibility of truth or absolute value; nothing can be known with certainty, thus moral judgements become impossible.

Derrida once called deconstruction 'a certain experience of the impossible'. He undermined the supporting structures of the Western intellectual tradition. But is there any point in his so doing? Do we reason outside of a cultural/intellectual context? Can we reason if this context has been destroyed? If this context is inadequate should it not be corrected? Who is to correct it and from what standpoint?

Others have denied that Derrida's texts are either important or philosophical, maintaining that he has perverted a serious philosophical quest, depriving the mind of its defences against dangerous ideologies. But where do they locate the source and validity of such defences?

# Conclusion

In this brief history of Western philosophy you will (I hope) have come to appreciate the ideas with which philosophers struggle. You may also now feel in a position to say what philosophy is.

For **Socrates**, philosophy was mainly a matter of getting to grips with ethical problems; but he was convinced that to make correct choices one had to have correct knowledge. For him, ethics was a question of knowledge, so it also involved asking questions like 'how do I know?' and 'what do I know?' Socrates of course worked out his ideas in the hurly-burly of the world of his day. As indeed do all philosophers. They are not living in a cocoon protecting them from the problems all around them. Those problems are what started them asking questions in the first place. Socrates was puzzled by the dishonesty of those who claimed to teach the 'skill' of arguing both for and against the same position. He wondered what sort of 'truth' might be involved here. His method was to question.

**Plato** took the theory of knowledge further and developed his theory of the forms. This involved 'seeing' what might be the eternal and immutable form of things, what makes them as they are, keeps them as they are, what is involved in knowing them as they are. Plato's response was a mystical one, but its ramifications went far beyond the dry theory of knowledge; it involved thinking about the ideal society and more particularly the ideal state. From this flowed a series of reflections on human nature and human gifts, on how those gifts might best be used; on what is justice and on who should rule, how the state should be governed and what it means to govern oneself.

**Aristotle**'s approach tended to be more practical and less mystical than that of his teacher. It also tended to be more analytical. He loved to draw up vast lists of information so that he could adduce universal rules from it. It was as if he were saying, 'knowledge applies to what is universally true, but when we go looking for this truth we only come into contact with individual states and objects. How do I attain a universal knowledge out of a welter of individual happenings and things?' Aristotle was a 'systems' man. He wanted not only to know what was true, but why it was true. He wanted to set out the problem clearly, delineate the vocabulary appropriate to it. He tried to elucidate the principles by which things worked and to examine and describe them in an ordered and graded sequence.

After Aristotle came two thinkers who had a quite different temper of mind: **Epicurus** and **Zeno**. With them the focus of attention seemed to draw away from the community and concentrate instead on the individual. For Epicurus pleasure was the sole good. He advised living moderately but in accordance with pleasure. He addressed his advice to the individual; vast schemes of organizing and controlling society as a whole have been left behind. This was also the focus of Zeno, who again offered advice to the individual on how to achieve some form of salvation in a fragmenting world. These are philosophies of personal consolation, movements of withdrawal from a world which was experienced as painful.

By the time of **Thomas Aquinas** the world had changed considerably: the vast Roman empire had come and gone, and a new Christian civilization had been forged following the centuries of disturbance. The Church was now the main authority. Thomas Aquinas faced the situation of his day by establishing a synthesis between the recently rediscovered writings of Aristotle and the now well-established Christian faith. System was once again back on the agenda. Aquinas was considered to be an innovator; he laid Christian teaching on a foundation of philosophical reason. In theology there are certain things that can only be asserted and accepted on the basis of faith: notions such as the Trinity, the atonement and salvation, but with Aquinas they were wedded to a reasoned and critical system, in his case that of Aristotle. After Aquinas it was accepted that a philosophical system could provide the intellectual basis on which to place discussion of revealed Christian teaching. This outlook is still familiar today:

the philosophy of Heidegger providing such a foundation for a number of twentieth-century theologians.

**Descartes** placed the self right in the centre of philosophical speculation, not at its ethical heart, but as the foundation of how we reason about knowledge. His starting-point was doubt and he was convinced that the conclusions produced by that act of doubting could not themselves be doubted: to be absolutely certain, one must doubt absolutely everything, thus discovering that the person doubting absolutely everything is the only certain thing. From that irrefutable fact he went on to build up his system, step by step. As Descartes meditated, each truth was established by a particular piece of evidence; but so that each element can remain valid in time, Descartes needed an external reference to guarantee them. This he found in God.

The ideas of **Locke** and **Montesquieu** were central to the birth of the modern liberal state. The state is not an instrument for imposing a set of ideas, be they those of Church, charismatic leader, caste or economic class; rather it is the free association of free individuals. Locke and Montesquieu recognized that there are many dangers if we live without any social organization at all; so individuals have come together to agree a set of institutions to remedy such defects. Theirs was a minimalist idea of the state, but it also involved a delicate balance between the application of power on the one hand, and freedom from the external imposition of power on the other.

**Spinoza**'s basic idea was that of *substance*, which he held to be self-evidently true. He went on to argue that there is only one substance (God or nature) and that whatever is, is in God. When we speak of God we are thinking in terms of cause; when we speak of nature we are thinking in terms of product. Spinoza's system was mechanical and impersonal.

**Descartes** and **Spinoza** both contemplated examples of rationalist philosophy. Rationalist philosophers believed that the universe functions in a rational manner and that the underlying principle of this functioning could be known by using reason alone, the starting-point of such an outlook is logic and they applied techniques derived from mathematics.

With **David Hume** comes quite a different mode of thought. The empirical challenge was simple: all classical philosophies were built upon a foundation that assumes the existence and power of God. The empiricists pulled the theological carpet out from under the feet of classical metaphysics and then sat back waiting for the whole structure to collapse. Empiricists rested everything upon experience; we only know if we have a sense-impression of something (I know it is raining because I can feel the rain on my face, etc.) By applying this doctrine to the idea of cause, Hume made it ridiculous. We see this when we confront his conclusions with the results of scientific experiments; they have arrived at their verdicts by applying the very doctrine which Hume had denounced.

**Kant**'s thought was both a celebration of the success of science and a lively critique of empiricist thought. For Kant, the laws of nature described by science were not simply true and universal, they were *a priori*, that is to say necessarily true and universal. Science just does not happen to succeed; it succeeds because there is a hidden necessity which must be uncovered and explained. Philosophers must consequently understand why science succeeds, but they must also ask themselves if all morality, art and religion are eventually going to be subject to scientific methodology or if other forms of thought are autonomous, legitimate and indispensable.

**Karl Marx**'s approach to philosophy was quite different, yet his starting-point, like that of many another philosopher, was metaphysics. Marx denounced religion and put in its place a dynamic materialism. This functioned according to the dictates of the Hegelian dialectic: reality is not static; its course is one of rising progress, evolving with abrupt spectacular leaps. The change comes about through the class struggle and the evolutionary stages from feudalism to communism are inevitable. This is a philosophy of how society functions and changes.

If Marx was the prophet of the revolutionary masses, **Nietzsche** was the prophet of the exalted, defiantly independent 'new man'. He must will to power, rethink all values and aim to become superman. He must accept his condition alone in the world, must create his own values and style his life in accordance with his circumstances; he must despise weakness in himself and in others and triumph over limitation. Here is a philosophy of the stand-alone individual.

Analytic philosophy was born with **Wittgenstein**. This practice of philosophy has nothing to do with the dogmatic teachings of all the philosophers who preceded him and took its inspiration for methodology and argumentation from the sciences and logic. Wittgenstein held that in order to understand what he was about the reader would have to recognize something in his thought, to have already thought the same thing, possibly without being aware of it. His focus was on language and on how to analyse it: two philosophies of how language functions. Analytic philosophy tends to see all philosophical problems as problems of language. It is a theory of the limits of what can be said, and in part, of the limits of what cannot be said; though in spite of being told by so many thinkers what cannot be said, the human soul still seems intent on saying it.

What cannot be said returned with a bang in **Heidegger**'s philosophy of Being. Our being-in-the-world is not a simple inert presence; it is a total engagement and involves our transcending the world which is itself inhabited by a transcendence which exists. Our existence is a being-with inhabiting the world in co-presence with other transcendent presences in the world. One must be conscious of Being, the fact of being which causes beings, rather than nothing, to be; Being is distinguishable from beings, which just are. Traditional metaphysics had, according to Heidegger, forgotten Being. By refusing to distinguish between Being and beings, metaphysics had, through its own wilful negligence, become the science of beings, mere objects amongst others.

**Sartre**, a philosopher of the absurd, took metaphysics in a new direction; rather than using it to create an order, he used it to demonstrate the total impossibility of preordained order and the absurdity of an order created by ourselves. We can only exist by adopting a meaning and purpose we have made up for ourselves. Whatever meaning we bring to our existence is in no way better than any other meaning we could have invoked. Our problem is that we cannot exist without any sense of meaning at all. We cannot do without meaning and no meaning adequately fulfils the function that meaning ought to have in our lives. There is no purpose to our existence yet we have to decide how to give it the purpose which is impossible. Absurd!

Finally we come to a philosopher of the meaning of the text. **Derrida** emphasized that language cannot refer to a fixed stable meaning. His term, 'deconstruction', is used to unravel meaning from texts in order to show that it is composed of assumptions that cannot be true; the meaning of the text cannot be limited by the intentions of the author of the text. Western philosophy has been obsessed with the search for reliable meaning; Derrida held that the quest was a false one. Words do not carry meaning with them, they 'put off' their ability to carry meaning by referring to other possibilities of meaning. Language is relational.

We have now moved away from a 'modern' view of the world, where reality was restricted to the observable system of nature, the human was the highest value, the scientific method was considered the only one suited to gaining knowledge. The modern outlook believed in progress, individuals being independent and free, objectively weighting up evidence, deciding for themselves, liberated from the conditioning imposed by their own place and time. The modern person knew things as they were, all external authority was suspect and subjected to deep examination.

In the late twentieth century humanity is held to have adopted a mindset sometimes labelled 'postmodern'. Here the objectivity and certainty of knowledge are denied. It is impossible to construct all-inclusive systems of metaphysical, religious or historical explanation. The postmodern individual refuses to accept that knowledge is inherently good; belief in progress has been abandoned. Truth is increasingly known through channels other than reason – intuition for instance – and truth and knowledge are often seen as the accepted beliefs of a particular community.

These are very general, sweeping statements, but perhaps you can see the role Derrida played in their slow, surreptitious, fragmentary acceptance.

So people have been practising philosophy for over 2500 years, yet they still haven't managed to agree precisely on what philosophy is. Philosophy, we might say, involves a strange mixture of scientific, theological, mystical and ethical reflection on the nature of the world we live in, our place in it and whether there might be any ultimate purpose to our existence. What is common to all thinkers and systems is 'reflection'. The earliest writers assumed that by thinking deeply and consistently, the nature of things would be revealed. Later thinkers argued that philosophy involves not only reflection about the world, but also observation and practical experiments. Still later thinkers maintained that analysis is concerned with the use of language and that analysing how it functions was a prerequisite for philosophical reflection. Then came the suggestion that no text has meaning until read by readers, who, by bringing their own concerns, assumptions and intuitions, subtly alter what the text may have set out to say; thus meaning is not predetermined, but potential.

Rather than trying to say what philosophy is, this book has been concerned to show what these philosophers have done. Philosophy is less a body of knowledge and more of an activity. Its distinguishing trait is the use of logical and disciplined argument. One of the reasons people come to philosophy is to 'find wisdom'. (Don't raise your expectations too high!) One of the reasons people stick with philosophy is that, once they start to analyse and classify ideas, they are dissatisfied with what they have discovered and wish to make improvements. Thus philosophy has both a critical and a constructive function.

Philosophers think and argue about the sort of things most of us take for granted in our everyday lives: 'the meaning of life', right and wrong, politics, the nature of the world around us, the nature of our perceptions of that world, mind, art, science. They question fundamental beliefs: why is it wrong to kill, to steal or to lie? Are there occasions when it might conceivably be right to perform such actions, and in what circumstances? where do you draw the line, and is that a legitimate question? The study of philosophy helps us to think clearly about our prejudices, about why precisely we believe what we do. We study philosophy because we believe, with Socrates, that the unexamined life is not worth living; because thereby we learn to think; because it gives us pleasure.

Philosophers always seem to be arguing over questions they cannot answer. There are two ways of thinking about that problem: either to say it is not permissible to ask such a question (a most illiberal and unphilosophical approach); or to go on asking the question in different ways, shifting the analysis and re-evaluating the status of the question. There is never any guarantee that the answer we find is going to be the one we want. Nearly all philosophy has to do with dissatisfaction with old ideas and an urge to find new ways of looking at questions or solving problems. Philosophy may be both reflective and transformative.

Philosophy involves an element of metaphysical speculation and another element which is a critique of what we know and believe, how we judge what we know and believe and how we judge the processes which lead us to knowledge in the first place. But philosophy also has to do with values. Perhaps even if you are not in a position to say what philosophy is you may at least be able to say what aspects of philosophy interest you.

I hope the quest continues. Good luck!

# Further Reading

My first suggestion for further reading, strange though it may seem, is a series of cartoon books on philosophers and philosophical subjects. Icon Books publish an 'introducing' series on Aristotle, Derrida, Descartes, Heidegger, Kant, Marx, Nietzsche, Plato, Sartre and Wittgenstein. These also extend to branches and subjects, such as critical theory, empiricism, ethics, existentialism, logic, Marxism, modernism, political philosophy, postmodernism and the Enlightenment. They are serious books written by specialists for the general reader in a slightly zany manner. The cartoons often make the point more strikingly than the text. See www.iconbooks.co.uk.

Oxford University Press's Past Masters series of introductions to various thinkers are also useful. Philosophers covered include Aristotle, Aquinas, Descartes, Hume, Kant, Locke, Marx, Montesquieu, Plato, Spinoza, Wittgenstein and Socrates. Fontana Modern Masters (London: HarperCollins) is a further series of introductory books. There are titles on Derrida, Heidegger, Marx, Nietzsche, Sartre and Wittgenstein, among others.

For other reading on the philosophers featured in this book see:

Appelbaum, D., *The Vision of Hume* (London: Shaftesbury, Element Books, 1996).

Brickhouse, T.C. and Smith, N.D., *The Philosophy of Socrates* (Oxford: Westview Press, 2000).

Caputo, J.D. (ed.), *Deconstruction in a Nutshell: A Conversation with Jacques Derrida* (New York: Fordham University Press, 1997).

Caputo, J.D., *Demythologizing Heidegger* (Indianapolis, IN: Indiana University Press, 1993).

Copplestone, F.C., *Aquinas* (London: Penguin, 1955).

Grayoff, F., *Aristotle and his School* (London: Duckworth, 1974).

Hollingdale R.J., *Nietzsche, the Man and his Philosophy* (Cambridge: Cambridge University Press, 1965).

Kenny, A., *Descartes: A Study of his Philosophy* (Cambridge: Cambridge University Press, 1968).

Körner, S., *Kant* (London: Penguin, 1955).

Love, N.S., *Marx, Nietzsche and Modernity* (New York: Columbia University Press, 1986).

McGuinness, B., *Wittgenstein: A Life* (London: Duckworth, 1988).

Murdoch, I., *Sartre, Romantic Rationalist* (London: Collins/Fontana).

Nichols, A., *Aquinas, an Introduction to his Life, Work and Influence* (Grand Rapids, MI: Eerdmans, 2003).

Quinton, A., *Hume* (London: Phoenix, 1998).

Ritchie, D.G., *Plato* (Bristol: Thoemmes Press, 1993).

Scruton, R., *Spinoza* (London: Phoenix, 1998).

Sharples, R.W., *Stoics, Epicureans and Sceptics* (London: Routledge, 1996).

Woolhouse, R.S., *Locke* (Brighton: Harvester Press, 1983).

The following books deal with general philosophical problems rather than individual philosophers.

Ayer, A.J., *The Central Questions of Philosophy* (London: Pelican, 1973).
— *Philosophy in the Twentieth Century* (London: Unwin, 1982).

Deleuze, G. and Guattari, F., *What is Philosophy?* (New York: Columbia University Press, 1994).

Honderich, T. (ed.), *Philosophy Through its Past* (London: Penguin, 1984).

Morton, A., *Philosophy in Practice: An Introduction to the Main Questions* (Oxford: Blackwell, 1996).

Teichman, J. and Evans, K.C., *Philosophy, a Beginner's Guide* (Oxford: Blackwell, 1991).

So far as history of philosophy is concerned, Bertrand Russell's *History of Western Philosophy* (London: George Allen & Unwin, 1946) is a useful guide, as is F. Copplestone's *A History of Philosophy* 9 vols (London: Continuum, 1962).

# Index